The 12 STAGES of HEALING

Also from Donald M. Epstein

Healing Myths, Healing Magic

The 12 STAGES *of* HEALING

A NETWORK APPROACH TO WHOLENESS

DONALD M. EPSTEIN
with
NATHANIEL ALTMAN

AMBER-ALLEN PUBLISHING

NEW WORLD LIBRARY

Co-published by Amber-Allen Publishing and New World Library

EDITORIAL OFFICE:
Amber-Allen Publishing
P.O. Box 6657
San Rafael, CA 94903

DISTRIBUTION OFFICE:
New World Library
14 Pamaron Way
Novato, CA 94949

Editorial: Janet Mills
Cover design: Kathy Warinner
Text design and typography: Stephanie Eichleay
Illustrations: Richard Capra
Backcover photo: Jackie L. Epstein

Library of Congress Cataloging-in-Publication Data
Epstein, Donald, M., 1953–
    The twelve stages of healing : a network approach to wholeness /
by Donald M. Epstein, with Nathaniel Altman.
    p.   cm.
Includes bibliographical references
ISBN 1-878424-08-4
        1. Chiropractic. 2. Healing. I. Altman, Nathaniel, 1948-. II. Title.
RZ241.E67 1994   94-21081
6615.8'52—dc20   CIP

ISBN 1-878424-08-04
Printed in Canada

Distributed by Publishers Group West

20 19

Dedication

This book is dedicated to my wife, Dr. Jackie L. Knowles, for her gentle strength, support, friendship, love, guidance, and understanding through all my Twelve Stages of Healing. Thank you for helping me with my longest journey, the path from my head to my heart.

Table of Contents

Chapter 1   7
Stage One: SUFFERING

Different from pain, suffering is marked by a profound awareness that "something is wrong." Parts of our being have been
separated from our Inner Self — the core of our being. This
especially occurs when we are confronted with a traumatic or
chaotic event or loss. The lesson of this stage is the acceptance
that nothing works at this time; we are presently helpless.

Chapter 2   23
Stage Two: POLARITIES AND RHYTHMS

The awareness that suffering involves cycles, polarities, and patterns is the essence of this stage. It begins with the search for the
"magic genie" who will save us from our distress, pain, or crisis. We try to gain power over our helplessness through external
authorities, procedures, and treatments. Eventually, as we heal,
we see that our genie is not so magical. We become aware of
our rhythms and polarities, and discover that we are partially
responsible for our distress.

Chapter 3   43
Stage Three: STUCK IN A PERSPECTIVE

This stage of healing involves the recognition that our distress is
associated with being stuck in a perspective. Our concepts or
our physiology have been fixated. We don't need to know why
we've been stuck, or what to do about it. We just need to have
the simple awareness that we've been stuck.

This stage of healing is one in which we realize that the "script" determined by the above three stages is no longer desirable or no longer works. Initially, we are angry that we have lost our power and are determined not to let it happen again. As we progress through this stage, we no longer choose to dishonor ourselves.

This stage is associated with having a strong enough sense of self to merge with the illusion which keeps us from our "light" or our "shadow." With merging, the part of our nature we have alienated, disliked, or ignored is integrated into the rest of our being to create more wholeness.

In Stage Six we build momentum and flexibility. The alienated, traumatized, denied or redirected consciousness or energy is being prepared for discharge and resolution. We feel the tension building within ourselves as this process advances, and find ways to create change and improve flexibility to continue the process.

This stage may involve a discharge of the muscular system, such as movement of the extremities, or processes such as fever, coughing, sneezing, crying, screaming, and laughing. When the discharge occurs after the previous six stages, and a sense of accomplishment, peace, and inner strength accompanies the process, then resolution has been achieved.

After the resolution and discharge we are emptied. This is not a space of nothingness, but instead a place of possibilities. We enter into a state of gratitude, vulnerability, connection with our external rhythms, and alignment with events around us. We expect serendipity to be available for us as a natural way of life.

Chapter 9   149
Stage Nine: LIGHT BEHIND THE FORM

From our place of emptiness and gratitude we become aware of our fullness of light and energy. We experience that we are more than our physical body, and actually become aware of the flow of life force through and around us. We may even experience our energetic connection to others. This occurs in conjunction with awe and joy for the process.

Chapter 10   165
Stage Ten: ASCENT

There is an awareness of Being — not as an intelligent being, but as intelligence itself; not as housing a Spirit, but as Spirit itself. We experience our union with the creative force of the Universe. We transcend all limits, boundaries, language, judgment, and our existing sense of self. We receive the gift of knowing the oneness of all creation, and gain immense wisdom during this stage.

Chapter 11   183
Stage Eleven: DESCENT

We are renewed beyond our limits and sense of self and enter into the world again. We know that we are part of all we perceive and responsible for what we know. We live without being attached to our situations. We love and serve life and others. We communicate with ourselves and others through our wounds instead of from them.

Chapter 12   197
Stage Twelve: COMMUNITY

We experience our involvement with humanity and recognize that wholeness comes from bringing our gifts of individuality into community. We recognize that all of our choices are spiritual ones and affect the entire globe of beings. Eventually we realize that the limits of what we can bring to community stems from our own lack of wholeness. Therefore we seek to re-experience the rhythm of the earlier stages.

Acknowledgments

I am grateful for this opportunity to thank some of the numerous people who have assisted me in my process, supported the model of healing referred to in this book, and helped in this project.

To my parents, Marion and Carl Epstein, who have given me the gift of life, taught me compassion and love for all living creatures, and created the space for me to hear and speak my truth of the moment. To my children, David and Debra Epstein, and to Daniel and Louise Knowles, for being part of my family, giving me such *nachas* (joy only a parent would know), and helping me know that there is hope for humanity.

To Louise and Jack Haskell for their love and support, and for their greatest gift to me, their daughter, Jackie Louise, my wife. To Jackie for being who she is and for her brilliance, humor, warmth, love, and commitment.

To my brother, Roy, for a special childhood, friendship, and understanding even over great distance. To Sue, Keith, and Margot Epstein for being part of my family. To my late Uncle Jules for teaching me about the magic of humor.

To Alison and John Michael for all their love, guidance, and tireless work that provides me with more effective and creative time. To Johnny and Jaclyn Michael for adding more fun to the family. To Norma Michael for her assistance in making my life easier. To Kathy and Jimmy Nimark, Mariah Wooster, Michael Canale, and Keri Lewin for being part of our community.

I want to express my gratitude to those I have adjusted over the years, to those who have taught me about all stages of healing as they moved through their processes, to the dedicated members of the Association for Network Chiropractic and their practice members who, by participation in their healing, are creating the space for others to experience healing in their lives.

To Dr. Thomas Whitehorne, Dr. Martin Greenberg, and Dr. Frank De Giaciamo who ignited the gentle spark within me during my chiropractic education. To Dr. Bob Verna and Dr. Stanley Alpert who nurtured the development of my humanity as a newly practicing chiropractor. To Dr. Pasquale Cerasoli, whose ideas popped into my consciousness years later. To Vincent Sica, who taught me to surrender and listen to Spirit and to seek my union with God. To Drs. Thom and Betty Gelardi for their unswerving dedication to chiropractic, their serving of humanity, and their unconditional parental guidance and love.

To Dr. Arno Burnier and his wife Jane for their love and vision. To Dr. Gerald Clum for his friendship, understanding, and trust. To Dr. Jim Parker and Dr. Karl and Judy Parker for their support of leading edge concepts in healing. To Nick Gordon for his personal guidance, support, and insight into fostering community. To John and Deo Robbins, Peter G. Massey, Mildred Aissen, Alice Winholtz, Peter Wellstood, Sandra Michael, Dale Halaway, Dr. Gary and Emily Dunn, Drs. David and Susan Breitbach, Drs. David Tribble, Michael Stern, Sharon Williams Stern, Lawrence Conlan, Janine Dobson, Graham Dobson, and Ralph Boone for their help with reading and suggestions in the manuscript. To Don Campbell for his trust, guidance, vision, and friendship. To Richard Capra for his wonderful artwork and patience.

To Drs. Lance Wright, Lorrie Eaton, Richard Kaye, Gabriel Russo, Vincent and Rosemarie Monaco, Lucinda Weeks, Alan Weingrad, Larry Zaleski, Sue Brown, Jan Kirschner, Robert Edelhauser, Donna Mutter, Wayne Rebarber, Fred Kingsbury, Robyn Graber, Scott Simerman, Jeff Bueno, Steven Wechsler, Judy Scher, Charlie Hilston, Renee Sexton, Thom Rogers, Linda Capra, Henri Marcoux, Lasca Hospers, Rick Moss, Imants de la Cuesta, Donald Glassey, Mark McDougall and wife Debra, Seth Friedman, Mark Haverkos, Ted Robinson, Esq., and Gillam Kerley, Esq., who are working with me teaching, presenting, or organizing seminars or guiding the development of the Association for Network Chiropractic. For all those who have helped in community with me who I may not have mentioned by name — thank you. You know who you are. Yes, you! Thanks.

Preface

In my work as developer of Network Chiropractic, I discovered that the healing process is made up of a sequence of twelve basic rhythms, or stages, of consciousness we pass through between "hell" and "heaven" in this lifetime. After observing thousands of people over a ten-year period, I discovered that each stage helps us reunite with aspects of ourselves that have been injured, betrayed, alienated, forgotten, abused, shamed, traumatized, ignored, or not forgiven.

I have always viewed integration and alignment as essential to the healing process, so I decided to call these rhythms "the twelve stages of healing." Although the stages are interconnected and interdependent, each one is also distinct, with its own rite of passage, which is often a chaotic experience known as a healing crisis.

Rites of passage form an integral part of many indigenous cultures around the world. They assist and support members of the community through important life changes like birth, puberty, marriage, illness, and death, and are especially important during periods of crisis. But contemporary Western society has lost sight of many of these rites, so that we must create our own rites of passage, especially as they pertain to health and healing.

The Twelve Stages as Rites of Passage

Have you ever wished you could marry a prince or princess, attain gold and jewels beyond your dreams, live in a magical kingdom, communicate with animals, be respected for your wisdom and leadership, accomplish feats of bravery and skill, and live happily ever after?

You may say, "I'd love to experience these things, but they only happen in fairy tales and myths. They don't happen in my life. After all I've been through. . . After enduring so much hardship. . ." These are some of the statements we make to justify our not having realized our most cherished dreams. Yet, in fairy tales, biblical stories, and heroic myths, the characters are forced to endure the entire spectrum of seemingly impossible, tragic, depressing, unjust, or frightening situations and are nevertheless able to achieve their hearts' desires. The heroes and heroines of these stories and myths are able to overcome their seemingly hopeless situations and transform their lives completely.

Such tales — with both their splendor and their tragic aspects — can teach us about the twelve stages. The stages reflect the rites of passage the heroes and heroines went through. By using their experiences as guides, we can learn the lessons they have to teach us — the essential pulse, rhythm, or consciousness of each stage — to experience a greater degree of wisdom, integration, and wholeness.

To quote the psychologist Bruno Bettelheim in his acclaimed book *The Uses of Enchantment: The Meaning and Importance of Fairy Tales,*

> The fairy tale is therapeutic because the patient finds his *own* solutions, through contemplating what the story seems to imply about him and his inner conflicts at this moment in his life. The content of the chosen tale usually has nothing to do with the patient's external life, but much to do with his inner problems, which seem incomprehensible and hence unsolvable. The fairy tale clearly does not refer to the outer world, although it may begin realistically enough to have everyday features woven into it. The unrealistic nature of these tales (which narrow-minded rationalists object to) is an important device, because it makes it obvious that the fairy tales' concern is not useful information about the

external world, but the inner processes taking place in
an individual.

Bettelheim's perspective on fairy tales is parallel to my understanding of disease and suffering: both are agents of healing when
viewed as perfect creations of disconnected, misdirected, or blocked
consciousness. Like the fairy tale, disease does not refer primarily to
the outer world, but rather to a disturbance in the bodymind's internal communication network. Diseases, symptoms, or distressing situations in our physical and emotional makeup are expressions of
inhibited, misdirected, or conflicting rhythms within the bodymind.
They create the need for us to look (although usually not consciously) at all our energetic resources and pathways.

Rather than being seen as a form of punishment or bad luck, disease or symptoms are essentially wake-up calls indicating that something is not right. They tell us we need to learn from what may have
led to disease — such as our thoughts, habits, and relationships —
thus enabling us to move on and redirect our lives. And, in choosing that new direction, healing can occur.

The twelve stages of healing offer support and understanding
while we encounter the rites of passage that make up the healing
process. Like a trusted friend, ceremony, or story, they are designed
to guide us gently through periods of transformation and change.

Mastering the Lesson of Each Stage

The key to mastering the lesson of each stage is to *get into* its
rhythm rather than to try to *get out of it*. You need to learn the lesson of that stage — not think or rush your way through it or deny
your way out of it. You need to recognize that your experience —
whatever it may be — is valid, even if you do not understand it at
the moment.

The stages of healing can be seen as a spiral path wide enough
for both ascent and descent. Each healing stage has a rhythm that
imparts its wisdom, and you will naturally progress to the next stage

once you have fully experienced the stage you are in. Each stage unfolds from the healing you have done, since you cannot heal what you have not yet dealt with.

If stages are missed or by-passed, your chances of "slipping" on the healing path are greater because you will not yet be flexible enough to deal with the new information inherent in each stage. For this reason, it is best to journey through each stage in its natural sequence. The lessons of each stage build upon one another, and each stage builds toward wellness.

Moving Through the Stages

Have friends ever told you to meditate when you felt that you were simply too tense to follow their advice? Has someone ever offered you a magical cure for your condition, but you wanted to find your own solution? Have you ever wanted to yell or scream at someone, but decided not to because it was "not the time"?

You most likely were correct in making your decisions, because you had an inner knowledge of the rhythms of the twelve stages. It is not time to meditate when you are not healed enough to do it. It is not time to express anger at your partner when you know it is really your issue. There is a time for embracing each stage and a time for relinquishing it. There is a time when it is safe to move to the next stage and there is a time when you have not developed the internal tools to negotiate the next stage. Healing involves *your* uniqueness, *your* rhythm, *your* timings. This book honors your awareness of when to, and when not to, move on.

One stage may clearly define your present reality, or you may say "That's me" in several stages. Most people will find considerable parallels between each stage and experiences they have had. This book is designed to help you understand the vocabulary of the rhythms that shape your reality and healing. Discover the stage with which you most identify. This is the stage at which you will begin your lessons. Follow the exercises closely and be willing to experience that stage. Life does the rest.

As you recognize and work through the twelve stages of healing, your healing process will become a dynamic one. Whatever the time frame may be, your goal is simply to be with each stage, learn its lessons, and then automatically and effortlessly move on.

Breath, Movement, and Touch

Breath, movement, touch, and healing are all interconnected. We hold our breath when we are distressed and breathe more fully when we are relaxed and flowing with the moment. We can lie to ourselves through words and thoughts, but we cannot hide from our touch, our breath, or our movement. Our touch is true. Our breath is true. Our movement is true.

After observing thousands of individuals on their healing journeys, I have classified each of the twelve stages of healing with their naturally occurring breath, movement, and touch. To touch, breathe, and move a region of the body is to provide a mirror to the body-mind as a whole, which discloses its deeply held secrets and alienations. Memories not yet safe to be disclosed to us, and aspects of our bodies whose rhythms have not yet joined with the rest of the bodymind, will be resistant to our touch, to our breath into those areas, and to our natural movements of those regions. But through the characteristic breath, movement, and touch of each stage, we can promote a safe and effective merger of our component parts into an enriched, fuller existence.

At the end of each chapter are exercises that will enable you to embrace the rhythm of that stage and more easily learn its lessons. I suggest that you only do the exercises associated with the stage in which you feel you need more completion. The performance of these exercises often results in what I call "Somato-Respiratory Integration." Somato refers to the body in its present state with all its past history. Respiratory refers to the magic of breath with its ability to bring life to the cells.

The breathing should not be forceful, as to cause hyperventilation. Instead, breathe just deep enough to sense movement in the region of the body with which you are connecting. Do each exercise for one to two minutes maximum for each area that you are connecting with, unless the rhythm takes over and the process becomes automatic. In this case it will complete when it completes, without mental thought or suggestion.

Using this Book

The Twelve Stages of Healing was written to offer support to the broad spectrum of people pursuing healing. It is also written for chiropractors, physicians, bodyworkers, therapists, social workers, and other healing facilitators. I hope it will help you identify when your patients will benefit the most from your procedures, and facilitate the clinical changes you would like to see more consistently in your practices. By acknowledging your patients' stages of healing, you can make a substantial difference in their healing processes.

Because the twelve stage model involves twelve basic rhythms or stages of consciousness we experience in our lives, each chapter will tend to activate that stage of consciousness. Because there is a step-by-step progression in the twelve stages, it is advisable to read the chapters in order. If, as you read a chapter, you feel you are not "resonating" (or connecting) with that stage and have difficulty reading through the rest of the chapter, turn to the end of the chapter and practice the exercises before reading further. Each time you read this book, you will find new meaning and greater self-understanding as you navigate the spiral path of the twelve-stage healing process.

Donald M. Epstein, D.C.
Boulder, Colorado

INTRODUCTION

Healing and Curing:
Two Different Worlds

Healing has little to do with the removal of symptoms. Rather, it is an intimate and integrative process that encompasses every aspect of our being — the entire spectrum of our existence. Healing transcends the simplistic notion of jumping out of a hospital bed or getting up from a wheelchair and walking; it involves the harmonious alignment of the physical, emotional, mental, and spiritual aspects of our being and how we relate to the world. The result is a greater experience of wholeness, wellness, and soundness. And wholeness is the birthright of every living being.

In his essay "The Spirit in Health and Disease," psychiatrist Laurence J. Bendit spoke of healing as a process of rebuilding one's life anew from chaos and disorder:

> Healing is basically the result of putting right our wrong relation to our body, to other people and . . . to our own complicated minds, with their emotions and instincts at war with one another and not properly understood and accepted by what we call "I" or "me." The process is one of reorganization, reintegration of things which have come apart.

In this book healing and curing are not used interchangeably. The word heal traces its roots to the Anglo-Saxon word *hal*, which means "whole," "hale," or "hearty." Rather than implying freedom from disease, healing involves root concepts like wholeness and wellness. These concepts imply self-empowerment, alignment, and integration, which enable us to fully express our unique potential as human beings in all aspects of life. Healing is often an uncomfortable process, but always empowering.

As we heal, it may appear that we are coming apart at the seams when we begin to wake up to aspects of ourselves that we were unaware of or were unable to acknowledge. But as we begin the process of discovery, acknowledgment, and alignment, our entire being is given permission to change. Through the natural, automatic release of old thought patterns, blocked emotions, and rigid ways of being, a new sense of respect for all our aspects and rhythms comes about. This is similar to the subtle, quiet, yet purposeful opening of a flower. In healing, no new magic is put into us and nothing is taken out.

Curing, on the other hand, implies that someone is trying to eliminate our disease, symptom, or crisis, most commonly through medication, surgery, psychotherapy, or other modalities. In the words of Janet F. Quinn, Ph.D., R.N., professor of nursing at the University of South Carolina,

> Curing may be conceptualized as the elimination of the signs and symptoms of disease. Typically people enter the health care system when indicators of illness can no longer be ignored. The signs and symptoms will be treated with medication, or if the signs and symptoms are severe enough, hospitalization will ensue. If, after a certain course of treatment by surgery and/or drug therapy, the signs and symptoms no longer exist, then we say that the person has been cured.

Curing has an important role. It offers us the gift of time so we might better understand the deeper significance of our symptoms. Curing can also offer us a greater degree of comfort to facilitate the process of realignment and redirection. When used as a stepping stone or rest stop to healing, curing can be beneficial. However, the way curing is regarded today can often deny the possibility of healing rather than facilitate it. Curing as an attempt to control our experience generally interferes with our ability to move into the unsolicited experiences we need to restructure our lives. When this occurs, instead of propelling us forward, curing holds us back.

Healing leaves in its wake a sense of accomplishment, fulfillment, and empowerment. Curing does not. Healing considers our uniqueness. Curing does not. Healing involves surrendering control of our inner and outer experiences. Curing involves an attempt to control our internal and external environments. Healing promotes wholeness, an uninhibited expression of natural rhythms, and unprovoked forgiveness. Curing seeks to label the effects (not the causes) of disease, place blame, and give explanations and excuses for undesirable experiences.

The Spiritual Aspect of Healing

The spiritual side of human nature is an essential, yet often overlooked, aspect of the healing process. The word *spiritual* comes from the Latin *spiritus* and *spirare*, meaning "to breathe" or "to blow." Spirit is something that cannot be seen, but can be experienced. In the poetic words of an anonymous teacher,

> There is a force that is unfathomable, omnipresent, unnameable, and omniscient. This intelligent and loving force stands behind and guides the evolution of physical manifestation. Spirituality is the label used to describe what occurs when we connect with this source.

The source of spirituality has many names: Organizing Wisdom, Great Spirit, the Christ Within, the Atman, or God. Connecting with this source is an automatic process that often occurs when we least expect it. Rather than being the result of searching and seeking, spiritual truth occurs by removing the blocks that prevent our knowing it. It is like being in a dark room and opening the blinds to let the sunlight in. By opening to our spiritual nature, we open to the new and the unexpected. According to Ernest Kurtz and Katherine Ketcham in *The Spirituality of Imperfection,*

> Spirituality points, always, beyond: beyond the ordinary, beyond possession, beyond the narrow confines of self, and — above all — beyond expectation. Because the "spiritual" is beyond control, it is never exactly what we expect.

The spiritual aspect of healing involves tapping into the deeper levels of being where our innate intelligence resides. As we connect to our inner rhythms and greater sense of wholeness, we begin to experience the rhythms, wholeness, and interconnectedness around us, which eventually expands to include the entire human and planetary community. Holistic physician and psychiatrist George L. Hogben described healing in *Spiritual Aspects of the Healing Arts,*

> Healing may be defined as a miraculous unfolding of consciousness for one's being in the world. We learn who we are, what and who really matter to us, how to express ourselves fully and openly. Ultimately, the healing journey leads to an intimate union with God through the experience of the flow of God's spirit within. It is a slow, arduous passage, unique for each individual, filled with danger and risk, triumph and joy, and finally, peace, trust, awe, reverence, love, tenderness.

Healing: A Broad Scope

The approach to healing presented in this book goes beyond dealing with a health problem or a healing crisis. It can also be used to enhance your relationships, career, financial investments, dietary habits, spiritual life, approach to education, the goods and services you use, and the institutions and causes you support. It is not intended as therapeutic information for any physical or emotional condition.

If you feel you need assistance from a health professional at any point in the healing process, please seek help; in some cases, doing so may even prolong your life. But do not confuse curing with healing. After you have addressed your immediate health concern, and you are out of impending danger and feel more comfortable, I invite you to return to the Twelve Stage healing process and move along the spiral path toward wholeness.

1

STAGE ONE

Suffering

Right now, I am helpless. Nothing works at this time.

It may appear strange to begin a book about healing with a chapter on suffering. After all, suffering is perhaps the one aspect of life that, more than anything else, we try to avoid. Yet suffering has fascinated us since the dawn of civilization and has been a central theme in our religious and literary traditions for thousands of years.

The early Jews, Christians, and Muslims taught that suffering was an integral part of the human condition: if we are human, we are going to suffer. They taught that suffering is brought about by ignorance or a misconception about our true nature and is linked to wrong attitudes or actions. But they also acknowledged that suffering can lead us to seek the meaning of life and guide us to a deeper understanding of our place in the world.

According to Annemarie Schimmel in *Mystical Dimensions of Islam*, "Just as wheat is ground and kneaded and apparently mistreated until it becomes bread, thus the human soul can mature only through suffering." Among the mystics known as the Sufis, tribulations and afflictions have long been considered a sign that "God is near."

Suffering is also part of the Hindu and Buddhist traditions. The

7

Buddha taught that suffering was one of the Four Noble Truths that, if properly understood, can lead to spiritual enlightenment. The Sanskrit word for suffering is *duhkha*, and is derived from *du*, "unpleasant," and *kha*, the "axle-hole in a wheel," suggesting something that is out of alignment and does not function at its full potential. Like early Western teachings, the Buddha taught that suffering was due to a lack of knowledge. It is not shameful to experience suffering. Like other aspects of the human condition, suffering exists so that we may learn to be free of ignorance and recognize our true nature as spiritual beings.

Suffering is also a major theme of myths and legends. Many biblical stories are based on suffering. The escape of the Jews from Egypt, the suffering of Jesus Christ in the Garden of Gethsemane on the eve of his crucifixion (culminating with the crucifixion itself), and the often violent stories about Christian martyrs and saints all deal with intense and prolonged ordeals of suffering. Halos around the heads of individuals who became saints reflect the glory bestowed upon them for their spiritual achievements attained through suffering.

The central themes of nearly all our best-loved fairy tales have to do with suffering, as well. Whether it is the tale of Cinderella (who lost her mother and endured years of abuse by her stepmother and sisters), Sleeping Beauty (who was put into a deep sleep after getting stuck with a spindle), Rapunzel (who was imprisoned for years in a tower by her jealous mother) or Beauty and the Beast (where the Beast is rejected because of his hideous appearance), all deal with the world of suffering.

Many stories of suffering involve a main character being immersed in what is called "the dark night of the soul": a time of darkness, loneliness, despair, and abandonment in an endless void from which he or she cannot escape. Often, the individual feels completely lost (a popular image in fairy tales involves a character wandering aimlessly through a dark and dangerous forest), moving deeper and deeper into the darkness.

In many fairy tales and myths, the heroes and heroines are portrayed as helpless; they are totally at the mercy of forces they cannot control and are not able to free themselves from their oppression. When they enter the dark night of the soul, they become completely cut off from whatever previously existed for them. Their lives take on new dimensions with no possibility of recapturing the lives they previously led.

In the minds of those suffering, the stories portray not only someone who is in pain, but someone whose soul is crying out, "Stop it! Stop it! Set me free! I can't take it anymore!" And many who move through suffering — such as the story of Christ on the cross — feel that God has betrayed or abandoned them.

These stories, as well as countless operas, plays, dances, and poems, have endured because they portray individuals — both fictional and real — who encountered suffering, became involved with their suffering, and somehow emerged from suffering victoriously. In many of these stories, ordinary people do extraordinary things in the face of physical challenge and emotional hardship. By courageously moving into their suffering and emerging through the other side, they are transformed into heroes and heroines and give hope to us all.

The Difference Between Pain and Suffering

From our earliest years, we are trained to avoid, control, modify, or otherwise escape suffering. Whether the suffering is related to physical pain, a threatening disease, humiliation, the loss of a loved one, the fear of failure, or the lack of fulfillment, most of us would agree that suffering is certainly among the least-desired and most unpleasant experiences we go through.

Suffering is often linked with pain, yet they are not the same thing. Pain is an awareness of discomfort on physical, emotional, mental, or spiritual levels. By contrast, suffering involves the experience of dishonoring, denying, or alienating our "true self," the core of our being, the wellspring of our awareness and self-expression.

This dishonoring is often activated by painful experiences and our reaction to them, which often involves a gradual process of numbing, armoring, and escape. Over time, this distorted view of ourself and the world around us sets the stage for more suffering.

A person in pain views their illness as a possession: "I am a person with cancer." A person who suffers views their reality as inseparable from the condition or situation; they actually identify with it: "I am a cancer victim." In other words, there is no difference between the sufferer and the source of their suffering.

According to *Webster's Ninth New Collegiate Dictionary*, to suffer is "to be made to bear, to be the victim of, to put up with, to undergo or be subjected to; to allow; to experience pain or injury, to experience loss, deterioration, etc." A major aspect of this definition is the term "made to bear." When you are forced to bear something, you simply cannot escape it. You feel as though you are a victim. You just have to put up with it; there is no denying or escaping from your situation. Pain, on the other hand, is an awareness that change is necessary. The dictionary defines it as "an unpleasant feeling which you have in a part of your body because you have been hurt or ill" and "the feeling of deep unhappiness that you have when unpleasant or upsetting things happen."

Like suffering, pain simply cannot be avoided no matter how hard we try; it is part of the human condition. If we are alive, we must feel pain as a built-in warning mechanism — as an important wake-up call to tell us that something needs to change. When we touch a hot stove, the pain we feel prompts us to quickly withdraw our hand from the burner. During suffering, however, we experience a feeling deep inside that something is terribly wrong with our lives and that there is nothing we can do about it. The outer event activates a raw place deep within our being; we feel paralyzed, helpless, victimized, and obsessed with getting out of "it."

When we experience suffering, the following statements often come to mind:

"Something is really wrong."

"God, when will this stop?"

"I'm going to die."

"Why isn't anyone listening?"

"What if he (she) never comes back?"

"I can't stand this pain — it's killing me!"

"Nothing works."

"There is no way out."

"God, why don't you care?"

During Stage One, we are often obsessed with fear about what is going to happen or fear of repetition of what already occurred. Because we feel out of control of our experience, our normal defenses break down and unresolved feelings, perceptions, and relationships that were held in check now come bubbling to the surface. Like a small child who is ignored, these aspects of our consciousness (whether connected to organs, feelings, unresolved issues, or situations) have "temper tantrums" and call out for our attention. Suffering is the result. It speaks volumes about those alienated, disconnected, and dishonored aspects of our selves.

Developing a Sense of Self

In Stage One, we are not yet whole enough to recognize a distinction between our sense of self and our suffering. Our self is the essential part of our nature that makes us different from everyone else. According to Dr. Roberto Assagioli, the developer of psychosynthesis, "the self is acutely aware of itself as a distinct and separate individual." This concept often brings with it a sense of solitude or separation from the world around us.

Our sense of self is not so much based on all that has happened in our lives, as it is based on what we select, imagine, and remember. These memories include relationships with parents, teachers, siblings, and friends; childhood training and education; successes and defeats; and the wide variety of traumas, challenges, and joys we experience as part of being human. Our sense of self is due to the way we learned to react or respond to our environment. In the stage of Suffering, our sense of self is rigid and fixed. It is not open to change. Therefore, when change occurs, our true essence seeks to make us aware that something is wrong and that the self we have right now is not working for our greater good.

The Western psychological model states that our problems are derived from not having a well-defined or fully developed sense of self. Psychologists state that we need to improve our sense of self and often look upon people who relinquish self-image, possessions, relationships, jobs, or status as sick or weak because they don't have a strong sense of self. But in Asia, where the Eastern perspective of psychology and spirituality is dominant, these same people would be considered healthy. Rather than being looked upon as weak or ill, they would be praised for moving past an illusory sense of self that no longer worked in order to become more enlightened or healed.

Eastern meditative and esoteric schools seek to transcend the illusions that the Western model has integrated into a sense of self. Eastern psychology states that our problems, including health problems, are the result of having *too much* sense of self and that we must relinquish the illusion of a separate sense of self in order to be whole or healed. This relinquishment is an essential part of the spiritual process described by Dr. Aminah Raheem, the developer of a psycho-spiritual approach to healing known as Transpersonal Integration:

> A sense of separateness — from oneself, others and the environment — is replaced by an inner attunement to a great natural Order. Surrender to that Order — the final stage of all spiritual practice — becomes possible and appealing. A sense of well-being and integrity will automatically accompany these knowings.

When we surrender to the greater order, we become aware that the self we took to be "us" is actually very small compared with our connection to the rest of the universe.

Achieving a sense of "no-self" (or, in reality, a "new-self") is one of the most important goals of the healing process. We may call it a "new-self" because when we look upon who we thought we were, we say, "No, that wasn't me!" This achievement can only occur after we relinquish those aspects of our being that no longer work for us. For relinquishment to take place, we first must be "someone" before we can be "no one." We need to develop a clear sense of self before we can evolve to a more "self-less" state. Those who are in the stage of Suffering have not discovered (or need to rediscover) their true self, which occurs as they move through the stages of healing.

A Distorted Sense of Self

Suffering is a natural by-product of a distorted sense of self. When we identify with portions of our being and with circumstances, people, things, and ideas outside us, we are ripe for suffering. And to the extent our self-image is intimately identified with an object or event (be it an idea, person, or thing), we are more likely to suffer.

Many of us base our identity on parts of our bodies, such as our hair, face, figure, breasts, or penis. Thus, suffering takes place when we lose (or fear we will lose) whatever we have identified with. A woman who loses a breast to cancer surgery may suffer intensely because she feels she is no longer a woman. But, in reality, losing a breast does not make her less of a woman. It's when she identifies with the breast as part of who she is that suffering is bound to happen.

This does not make it wrong to identify with any part of our body, and at some points in our healing process we may need to do this. But when our sense of self is based on possessions or external things — like bank accounts, cars, country club memberships, roles, relationships, status, or even the clothes we wear — we lay the groundwork for more suffering. In a world of impermanence, possessions are often lost or stolen; our homes may burn, our cars may be stolen, or our businesses may fail. This doesn't mean we cannot enjoy having nice homes, good cars, or money in the bank, but to the extent that the image of who we are is connected to these things, their loss (or our fear of losing them) will cause suffering.

This is why for many people, the traumatic events of life — which often involve major losses — will trigger suffering. Through suffering, we often become aware that we were living an illusion we were not conscious of: the illusion that my Jaguar is me, that my marriage is me, that my full head of hair is me. And as long as we consider the illusion to be real, we will continue to suffer.

Our inner wisdom is telling us that something doesn't work anymore, that a perspective — a point of view — we have lived with is no longer real. Events involving illness or loss may cause pain in varying degrees, but our level of suffering is always related to how we *perceive* these events in our lives. Suffering is a way for our inner wisdom to remind us that we need to alter our perspectives. In Stage One, however, we cannot perceive it as a wake-up call because there appears to be no reason why we should endure such suffering.

The reality of our true self often tries to speak to us through our misconceptions. We will not realize this until the later stages of healing — when we become aware that we have dishonored our true essence by failing to recognize it.

A Distorted Perception of Time and Space

During Stage One, we lose touch with normal time-space perception — the rules of time and space are suspended. When we are suffering, we may ask, "Get the doctor." "Bring me my medication." "Call my chiropractor." The person who is assisting us goes to the telephone and returns two minutes later. To us it seems like an hour and we may ask, "What took you so long?" Time stands still. We not only experience suffering in the moment, but often our minds drift to what has happened in the past or what may happen in the future, eliciting a feeling of, "Oh my God — it's going to happen again."

In Stage One, time and space are warped, indicating that suffering is essentially a matter of mind or of consciousness. Therefore, resolution of suffering can only come from the same place: the mind or consciousness.

A Time to Surrender

Every cell of the body has a consciousness of its own, and every cell shares the consciousness of the body's community of cells. When we are suffering, a regional, distorted, or alienated consciousness is calling for our attention. We often have a vague perception that some aspect of us is dying and we feel a sense of urgency to save the suffocating part.

We are aware that somehow, in some way, we have experienced a violation or a dishonoring. When this occurs, an illusory reality is breaking through. Life is saying to us, "Grow up! Work as a team! Get it together. This old, separative consciousness doesn't work anymore."

In stories like "Hansel and Gretel," "Little Red Riding Hood," or "Dracula," many main characters die or are otherwise eliminated while the hero survives and is transformed. Psychologists like Bruno Bettelheim view killing and dying as symbolizing the death of aspects of human nature that no longer work for the story's main character: it is an aspect of the main character that has to die. And through the process of this "death," the hero "lives happily ever after."

"Dying" is an integral part of moving through suffering. In suffering we are given the opportunity to "die" to old, tired perspectives and attachments that keep us from moving on, and old images of self that no longer work for us. We die to relationships we no longer need, die to memories of the distant past, and die to expectations of the future. Former basketball star Kareem Abdul-Jabbar spoke of this consciousness in *New Age Journal*:

> Athletes die twice. When the sporting career is over, and
> the body doesn't do what it used to, and the fans stop

cheering, it is like a death . . . If you can't make the transition into another way of life, you're doomed.

Dying in Stage One involves surrendering to the suffering we feel without trying to escape from it. It is not an easy process, but we have no alternative. If we try to avoid suffering, it often becomes more intense, often showing up uninvited in different areas of our lives with more vengeance than ever, and lasting much longer than would otherwise be necessary.

When you simply surrender to the stage of Suffering and allow suffering to happen, an important shift in consciousness takes place. As you stop fighting and give over to the suffering, it envelopes you, it encases you. You may feel yourself shiver in agony. You may hold your heart for the heartache you feel and grip your stomach for the stomach cramps; you may grasp at your lungs for the breath you cannot find. You may feel you are about to die, and you may feel totally abandoned and in despair. You may imagine you are surrounded by chaos and feel a sense of disruption or loss of who you were. To quote Bernadette Roberts in *The Path to No-Self,*

> Here begins the cauterizing, the burning through to the deepest center of being, which is painful and shattering to all aspects of self. The deep deterministic reins of self-control have been taken away and the willpower that glued together this fragile unity has dissolved. From here on, the reins of our destiny are in the hands of a greater power. . . . With no place else to go, nowhere else to turn, we have no choice.

Like the Frankenstein monster, who was a stitched-together assortment of separate, dead body parts, we have aspects of ourselves that feel foreign to us. They are no longer flexible or alive. Like the monster, we are trying to live a whole, unified life, yet we do not have the ability to reconcile the parts that are isolated from each other and separated from the essence of who we really are. We want them excised, removed, taken from us now. The struggle that ensues is what suffering is about. Something is being lost, something is dying, something is deteriorating. This loss expresses itself as, "This pain is terrible." "I'm going broke." "I'm losing my partner." "I'm afraid I'm going to die." "Someone please help me!"

What we are losing is our relationship to the part of us that is no longer working; it is time for it to die. Our involvement with the illusions behind the part that cramps or hurts so much must die. Until information or energy in the part that no longer works for us dies or joins the rest of the body, the rest of us cannot truly live.

A Time for Acknowledgment

In Stage One, we resist suffering when we try to deny it, escape it, intellectually understand the significance of it, or otherwise distract ourselves from directly experiencing it. Often a well-meaning person will try to help you avoid suffering and may say, "It's not all that bad" or "Don't worry, you'll get over it." These comments can be very upsetting when you are suffering. There is an interference in the connection between the infinite You and the way you are living. You need to amplify the voice within that is attempting to tell you, "Wake up!" Your essence knows that something is wrong, and that is all that matters.

Someone may approach us with a form of new age rhetoric that says, "How did you create this problem?" "Take responsibility for it." "Don't you realize your negative thought forms are the cause of it?" or "Why don't you state some positive affirmations?" The more people approach us with this kind of unsolicited advice, the less tolerant we are of them, the more ill-timed we realize their remarks are, and the deeper our suffering becomes. There is a time for this kind of rhetoric, but it may be effective only at a later stage of healing.

You may have suffered the loss of a loved one and a friend says, "Oh, well, he wasn't all that good to you anyway" or "Things will work out in time." No matter how wonderful that friend is, you have nothing but anger and animosity toward her. Why? Because when someone tells you that your problems can be solved rationally or reasonably while you are in the stage of Suffering, it's infuriating and simply not believable.

Logic or linear reasoning does not work when you are suffering. Only one thing works, and that is being acknowledged that you are suffering: "Your situation appears terminal. It appears that there is no way out. No one can help you. You are experiencing the most horrendous experience anyone can have." Another person confirming that something is indeed very wrong and that you feel violated is exactly what you are seeking.

When others acknowledge the critical nature of your situation, you feel a sense of peace. When they acknowledge your suffering and despair, they are helping you find resolution with the only spiritual and mental reality that can help liberate you. This reality is, "Nothing is working now." "I am helpless."

Seeking Help

During Stage One, it is sometimes necessary to remove pain and suffering through medication, surgery, and other procedures. Although many people can deal with the pain and helplessness of suffering on their own, some have lost control of their experiences to the extent that emergency medical treatment is not only appropriate, but is necessary to save their lives.

If you honestly feel you must get professional help from a therapist, a physician, chiropractor, or other healing facilitator during suffering, do so. For those who are moving through suffering, emergency treatment not only acknowledges their helplessness, but also provides both the time and the momentum needed to continue through the next stage of healing.

Many people in the stage of Suffering find the concepts of holistic health, alternative medicine, meditation, or transpersonal work confusing and unnecessary. And in the first stage of healing, they are probably right to resist them.

Upon visiting a doctor, they may hear something like, "You have such and such disease, and people rarely recover from it." You may feel that such responses are cold, insensitive, and the antithesis of healing. But for someone in the stage of Suffering, these responses are the perfect prescription. The simple acknowledgment of their helplessness in Stage One is most often enough for the sufferer to begin completion of this stage.

In my chiropractic office, I would often tell my new patients that there is nothing I can do to end their suffering. I would say something like, "There is nothing I can do for your pain. I will remove nerve interference from your nervous system, which coordinates all body parts and functions, but I don't know what that will do for your pain, if anything. You may choose to get emergency treatment for your pain." By my making such statements and acknowledging the potential lack of change in their situation, many people would immediately shift into Stage Two of healing.

During Stage One, a practitioner can either try to treat the disease or symptom or choose to work with the person who is suffering. But there is nothing a health practitioner can do to stop the suffering, except to help the person who is going through it. The actual suffering is an internal spiritual or mental emergency and cannot be effectively treated or cured. Understanding this concept can make all the difference in furthering the healing process.

Moving Through Stage One

The most appropriate response to Suffering is to stop thinking about its causes. During this stage we cannot perceive the problem yet. But by merging with the rhythm, vibration, or essence of suffering — without trying to figure out what to do, without making ourselves out to be right or wrong — by merely acknowledging the experience, we empower ourselves to maximize the experience of suffering.

We are not a person experiencing suffering; all we experience is the loss, all we experience is the pain, all we experience is the injury.

As we give ourselves over to the suffering, we are no longer in time, but are in a space between our thoughts, a space between the contractions and the pain, a place of not being alive, yet not being dead: we are just *suffering*.

The terror, violation, and helplessness we feel have an eerie life that in some form wraps itself around our distress. We may not understand it, and there is no rational way to perceive it. But we soon discover that on top of the physical or emotional pain, the suffering has a rhythm of its own. And when we resonate with the rhythm of suffering, that rhythm overtakes us and we move within it.

If we find ourselves shaking, rocking, twisting, or holding the affected parts of our bodies, we need to let this happen. It is like listening to a musical composition without thinking about it or trying to figure it out intellectually. We simply become immersed in it. After a while we become one with the rhythm and get to know the theme.

At that point, an important shift takes place in our being and we advance to another stage of consciousness. As if by magic, we find ourselves walking, climbing, floating — or otherwise transported — through a kind of corridor or doorway into a new stage of healing. We may emerge feeling raw, disheveled, vulnerable, and hurting, but we now perceive that we broke through a barrier that had kept us imprisoned. We begin to identify with the hero, the heroine, or whatever method that makes us feel better. We now begin to enter into the second stage of healing.

Hearing Yourself Ask for Help

In the despair of Stage One, you may ask for or pray for help, although you do not really expect it to make a difference. Therefore, you may say something like, "God, Oh God" without saying what you want specifically. After all, you don't expect it to make a difference anyway. You may say "God, help me!" but you cannot begin to focus on what the specific help would be.

Stage One Exercise

Lie on your back, or be seated. Touch your upper chest with both hands, palms facing downward, and breathe slowly in through your nose and out through your mouth. Breath only deep enough to feel your breath meet the rhythm of your chest rising and falling. Repeat this process for one to two minutes. If you find this painful or very uncomfortable, or if this exercise brings up intense emotions, continue for as long as possible until you need to stop.

Now do the same exercise with your hands placed at the bottom of your breastbone and breathe the same way. Then place your hands on your abdomen (near your navel) and repeat. Remember to breathe into the area where your hands are placed.

If you are in the stage of Suffering, you may find it physically difficult to firmly touch one of these regions and breathe into it. For those who may have unresolved Stage One issues, there may even be a high emotional charge or response during this exercise. If this exercise is very difficult to do in one of these regions, move to a different region that feels more comfortable. Let the peace you experience there spread to the region where you felt discomfort.

Stage One Declarations

When the breathing exercise is almost complete, make the following declarations to affirm your movement with Stage One:

"Right now, I am helpless."

"Nothing works at this time."

Stage One Exercise

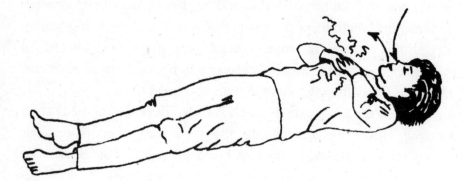

2

STAGE TWO

Polarities and Rhythms

There is a rhythm within me, and I am within this rhythm.

In Stage One, suffering was associated with having isolated certain aspects of ourselves — such as personality traits, diseased parts, painful memories, or unresolved childhood issues — from the rest of our bodymind. We may have been traumatized by an athletic injury or automobile accident years ago. We may have felt shameful about our "nasty" childhood sexual feelings, repressed the pain or guilt of a friend's death, or judged addictive behaviors as being either good or bad, acceptable or unacceptable. Suffering was the result of ignoring, denying, or redirecting the information these aspects wanted to share with us.

In the early part of Stage Two, the tendency to judge events and situations as good or bad intensifies. Rather than a person who is overwhelmed by the endless suffering of Stage One, we now have a greater "I" who makes judgments and evaluations about ourselves and life around us. In this stage our conversations often reflect these judgments and we speak in terms of a "bad back," "bum elbow," "lousy husband," or "horrible situation."

We are also likely to refer to the limbs and organs of our bodies

23

as if they weren't parts of us, and the health problems we are suffering from as if they are conditions that dropped on us from outer
space. "I caught the flu"; "My angina's acting up again"; "My arthritis is killing me" are characteristic of this mindset. Like the Frankenstein monster, in the early part of Stage Two, we still experience the
separateness of our body parts rather than experiencing these as
aspects of a fluid, interacting whole. We do not yet realize that this
alienated consciousness is the *source* of our suffering.

In early Stage Two, it is also common to blindly commit ourselves to procedures, rituals, therapies, and treatments. A woman
named Katie came to my office one day. Although she considered
her health to be generally good, she had felt a lack of energy since
undergoing a hysterectomy some months before, and she wondered
if Network Chiropractic would help. After several weeks of care, she
began to recall childhood memories of being raped by her stepfather.

Like many women who were sexually molested in their early
years, Katie had not yet come to terms with her trauma and the rage
and shame her abuse brought about. As a result, she alienated and
isolated the aspects of her bodymind that were connected to this
abuse. If we consider that the mind and the body are inseparable,
any consciousness that has not been acknowledged or has not been
truly seen, will make its claim for attention. In many cases it will
eventually manifest as a disease we can no longer ignore. And, as
with Katie, when the consciousness of these alienated aspects (tense,
armored, contracted regions) call for attention and resolution, gynecological problems like fibroid tumors, cysts, and painful menstrua-
tion commonly show up.

During the first and second stages of healing, many women who
suffer from such gynecological problems decide to undergo hys-
terectomies in order to rid themselves of diseased and damaged tissue and the part of the "self" that is judged as wrong, bad, or evil.
The problem is that although they remove the apparent source of
their suffering, they have not yet come to terms with the unresolved
memories, feelings, and patterns that may have contributed to the

physical problem. This is not to say that surgery is wrong or inappropriate. However, given the identical symptoms, true healing is more likely to occur in a later stage of healing when the patient is able to recognize and resolve the underlying issues.

A World of Polarities

In Stage Two, an important part of healing involves the awareness that there is a polarity within us, that some parts of our body-mind appear to have lives of their own, out of touch with the greater context. This polarity may be defined as a discrepancy between the whole body and an individual part. It may be experienced as an incongruous or dissonant rhythm, beat, or pulse in two or more regions of the body, and may show up as a persistent or chronic condition in any part of the body.

In the second stage of healing, our personality's involvement in polarity and judgment reveals that a sense of "me" is developing. After the bruising of our illusory self that occurs in Suffering, developing a sense of one's self is important. However, in Stage Two, as in many stages of development, it is possible to go to extremes as the pendulum of life swings in the other direction. We may have an internal dialogue that tells us there is a "me" in here and there must be something similar out there; I am good and what's out there is bad. Rather than see the "wronged" portion inside we experience the evils of life outside. We do not recognize that projection is occurring.

As we move out of Stage One into the early part of Stage Two, we have not yet claimed our inner power. Although we are moving in a direction toward empowerment and wholeness, our physiology is not developed enough to accept the power of our own self. Instead, we believe that someone or something outside of us will lead us out of our desperation.

In Stage Two, we often use outside agents — authority figures, law and order, miracle cures — to substitute for the inner power we have not yet claimed. It appears that life is a roller-coaster: always fighting, correcting or being corrected, saving or being saved, all by outside authorities, events, or procedures. Sometimes we question whether we have become "dramaholics" because extremes appear to dominate our lives.

Psychologists and physicians often make use of this aspect of Stage Two in their practices. For example, when patients begin therapy, they often have deficient or distorted senses of self. To remedy this problem, the therapist may have patients identify first with the therapist, who slowly gives back their power over the course of treatment. Patients project their problems, feelings, and ideas onto the therapist. As they begin to experience a clearer and stronger sense of self, they shift these projections from the therapist back to themselves so they can eventually resolve their issues by themselves.

The Magical Genie

In the early part of Stage Two, we are often tempted to seek a magical genie — a person, procedure, or thing — that will save us from feeling "bad" and will help us feel "good." This idea is similar to fairy tales like "Aladdin and His Wonderful Lamp" when a magical genie suddenly appears unsolicited. He usually offers the story's main character — who is often depicted as poor, downtrodden, and in intense suffering — three wishes. The story then examines the nature of the wishes, which at first glance are supposed to solve the sufferer's problems and fulfill his deepest needs.

> For two days Aladdin remained in the dark, crying and lamenting. At last he clasped his hands in prayer, and in so doing rubbed the ring which the magician had forgotten to take from him. Immediately, an enormous and frightful genie rose out of the earth, saying: "What wouldst thou do with me? I am the Slave of the Ring and will obey thee in all things."

This fairy tale instructs us about movement from Stage One into Stage Two. Once we surrender to the darkness and despair in Stage

One, a magical portal opens, consciousness shifts, and personal power becomes available, even if it appears from outside one's self.

In Stage Two, the magical genie may be a physician who will cure our disease or disability, a religious leader who will offer us enlightenment, or a new job that will provide us with prosperity and fulfillment. We may look for our Prince (or Princess) Charming who will make us feel loved and secure, or we may move to another part of the country (a magical kingdom) to begin a new life. In many cases we attract the people and situations that also resonate with this stage of healing.

Western culture makes it easy for us to seek power from outside sources. Advertising often portrays perfumes that are guaranteed to make us feel like a new woman or cars that will bring out the man in us. Drug companies offer a multitude of over-the-counter pills and potions to end our suffering, be it from headaches, menstrual cramps, itching, fatigue, diarrhea, intestinal gas, constipation, allergies, or colds and flu. Much of their advertising is geared to the Stage Two individual. It often portrays the medication going only to the sinuses, throat, stomach, or back, thus further reinforcing our perception of separateness.

The self-help marketplace offers thousands of courses and books on how to magically improve our lives, manage our money, and become a better lover. Spiritual teachers worldwide offer meditation techniques and religious practices that will free us from suffering, and promoters of diets and exercise offer programs guaranteed to make us thin, attractive, and happy. Even in politics we are conditioned to believe that a new leader will magically transform the economy and make things right for us.

For many who are in Stage Two, the modern medical establishment is a godsend. We have state-of-the-art hospitals staffed by teams of specialists who offer a dazzling variety of sophisticated diagnostic and therapeutic procedures: CAT scans and MRI machines, heart by-pass operations, organ and tissue replacements, and powerful drugs. Some of these therapies involve complex and

costly experimental procedures that are often sought by those suffering from potentially life-threatening diseases like cancer or AIDS.

For others in Stage Two, the magical answer may come from
gaining information: the newest and most extensive diagnostic test,
the insight into a personal medical history, or keeping up with the
latest medical literature. Again, we may find ourselves at a critical
time in our lives when medical intervention is the only way we can
continue in our healing process. An angioplasty, a coronary by-pass,
an appendectomy, or aggressive treatment to lower serum choles-
terol can often help us respond to the wake-up call a health crisis
can produce. And it can offer valuable time needed to move further
along in the healing process. Bernard S. Siegel, M.D., addressed this
issue as a surgeon in *Spiritual Aspects of the Healing Arts:*

> I . . . see my mechanical skills as a way of buying time
> for the healing process to happen. I know I can oper-
> ate on patients and see them have less pain and fewer
> complications when we are a healing team, utilizing
> faith in ourselves, our treatment and our spiritual faith.

Sarah's Story

Although Sarah had been taking nitroglycerine tablets to control
her chest pains for years, her son noticed that she was taking them
more often than usual and insisted she call her doctor. She was sixty
pounds overweight and rarely exercised, but her medication and
periodic visits to the cardiologist kept her symptoms under control.
Despite Sarah's protests that she was feeling fine, her doctor told her
son to drive her to the hospital.

After a few days of observation in the coronary care unit, Sarah
was told that she would have suffered a massive heart attack if she
had not gone to the emergency room. Her cardiologist scheduled an
angioplasty to clean out her arteries. The procedure took place later
that week without incident. She was grateful that the doctor had

saved her from a heart attack, and she left the hospital with high hopes for the future.

During the next couple of months, Sarah's life continued as before. Although she began to modify the amount of fat in her diet, she believed that the angioplasty (the magic genie) saved her from a heart attack (the evil villain). At the age of seventy-seven, she was happy with her life, and despite occasional chest discomfort she functioned fairly well.

However, during a follow-up exam, Sarah's cardiologist found that her arteries had clogged again. She was told that a second procedure would be more dangerous than the first, and if it wasn't successful, a coronary by-pass would be the only thing that could save her. Another angioplasty was scheduled. Like the first, it took place without incident. But as Sarah rested in the recovery room, she experienced a subtle shift in consciousness. She realized that the procedure was only going to buy her time until the next medical emergency. Although she hadn't made any decisions about her future, the second angioplasty was her wake-up call. She realized that her heart problems were bound to continue and would probably get worse. This understanding set the stage for her movement into the later stages of healing.

Seeking Help

As we can see in Sarah's case, therapeutic intervention is often appropriate in Stage Two. The suffering patient feels powerless and can only experience a sense of power by being "rescued" by someone else. To have an authority figure say, "Yes, in order to cure your cancer you'll have to undergo surgery, radiation, and chemotherapy" or "Yes, to treat AIDS we must give you these powerful drugs," can be very helpful — especially when such an experience inspires the patient to move to a higher stage of healing. The fact that many such treatments may be dangerous and even deadly is rarely considered (or if considered, rarely seen as a deterrent). It is "up to the genie" to know what is right.

Again, medical intervention may be appropriate at times, but it can serve as a pseudo-solution if the patient has not yet acknowledged or "merged with" the consciousness that created the suffering in the first place. By attempting to control our experience, curing can interfere with the ability to move through the chaos, discomfort, or particular experience we need to restructure our lives.

A *Feeling* of "*Being* Saved"

In Stage Two, we often feel grateful for our rescuer. Whether it was a physician who performed surgery, a chiropractor who delivered an adjustment, or a psychotherapist who offered understanding, we usually regard them as a hero who saved us from our problem. Our sense of self has not become strong enough for us to realize that we are doing the healing. We are only slowly becoming aware of the existence of the self that proclaims "You saved me."

In the past, we may have been fixated on our backs, our kidneys, our marriages, or whatever it was that distressed us so much. Rather than experiencing a sense of "The doctor stopped the pain," now the feeling is "The doctor saved me." A letter from a cancer patient is typical of this consciousness: "He [the doctor] helped me tremendously. He negated the effect of the chemotherapy and gave me inner peace."

One way we can tell we are involved in the Stage Two process is when we become aware of our relief and excitement over being rescued:

"Doctor, your treatment saved my life! I'll refer all my friends to you."

"I finally found my spiritual master. He brought me enlightenment at last!"

"I took this seminar and it changed my life."

"My new girlfriend is the woman of my dreams."

"The new baby saved our marriage."

"This diet plan is amazing! I'll never be fat again."

We often tell the world about how this doctor, this procedure, this medication, this guru, or this relationship saved us from the virus, the uncertainty, the ex-spouse (or the ex-spouse's attorney), that brought suffering to our lives.

The Bifurcation Point: Choosing a Direction

What usually happens at this point? The surgery fails to produce the results we expected, or the medication is less effective than the doctor hoped. We discover that the guru's meditation technique does not bring inner peace or that the new man or woman in our lives reminds us of the people we were involved with before. The arrival of the new baby intensifies our marital problems instead of resolving them. The new job may be worse than the previous one, or the new house is making us feel homesick for the one we lived in before. Dr. Yeshi Donden, who served for twenty years as the personal physician to His Holiness The Dalai Lama, spoke about this dynamic in his book *Health Through Balance:*

> Basically, every being on this planet . . . wants happiness and does not want any form of disease or suffering. Yet, we do not know how to achieve the causes of happiness and do not know how to get rid of the causes of suffering . . . . We make great efforts at techniques for achieving happiness and avoiding pain, but instead, mostly generate just the opposite of what we seek — bringing on ourselves more pain and suffering and diminishing whatever happiness we have.

We now discover that the people who rescued us weren't so perfect; their methods weren't foolproof. Perhaps we discover that what we thought were the causes of our problems weren't totally responsible after all. The hard and fast rules of good-bad, right-wrong become muddled, and we have a difficult time empowering both the cause and the solution we once held fast to. It is common for us to feel angry. We may be truly angry at ourselves, but because we are not whole enough to recognize this, we often blame the therapist, the physician, the guru, the product, or the procedure for failing to meet our expectations.

Upon reaching this juncture, we can choose one of two paths. One path involves looking for another doctor, another relationship, another place to live, or another job. We may decide to leave our newly-found religion and seek out a different one or say goodbye to the acupuncturist and find a psychotherapist. There is nothing inherently wrong with moving from one job to another or from one practitioner to another in any stage of healing. In order to look for the power we have not yet experienced, this choice may sometimes be necessary. Unfortunately, many people remain stuck in this cyclic process and do not use their experiences as stepping stones to help activate aspects within themselves that could give them greater wholeness.

I have found that most people fluctuate between stages One and Two for most of their lives. Rather than participate in a larger and more fluid rhythm that encompasses all the healing stages, they remain stuck in a vicious cycle of suffering and magical solutions.

The other direction we can take involves looking more closely at the situation and asking ourselves whether a pattern may be involved in our suffering. We begin to see a connection between our life circumstances and our ailments or troubles. Our cyclic involvement becomes more apparent. We may say to ourselves, "I went through this kind of suffering the last time my boss fired me" or "My wife is doing the same thing my ex-wife did at this point in our relationship."

Cycles and Rhythms of Life

The pulse of life is one of cycles and rhythms. There is a rhythm to the seasons and to the ocean tides; there are cycles in the growth of plants and in the course of night and day. Whether we speak of the life of a star, a planet, a tree, or a human being, there are observable cycles of birth, youth, maturity, old age, and death. There are cyclic movements to the female menstrual cycle, distinctive rhythms to the human heartbeat, and a rhythmic breathing pattern of the lungs. There are different rhythms to learning and working, as well as rhythms of emotional expansion and contraction.

The ancient Chinese practice of acupuncture — as well as the healing art of *Qigong* — are based on understanding the rhythmic pulses of energy in the body. If we look closely at our lives, we can discover a subtle, natural rhythm in our intimate relationships, as well as rhythms that connect us to other family members and friends.

These cycles and rhythms are changing all the time. Although our heartbeats have definite rhythms, they vary according to changes in our physical activities and levels of emotional stress. Although trees have normal cycles of growth, as shown in their yearly rings, they also reflect the challenges the trees must face during their yearly cycles like droughts, diseases, or fires. Each cycle is unique, and yet all cycles of life fit into an underlying form of rhythmic order and all respond to different conditions within the whole picture. In her book *Ancient Wisdom, Modern Insight*, Shirley Nicholson wrote,

> Nature and its numberless cycles might be compared to a great symphony with each cycle having its unique place in the ongoing rhythm of the whole. From cell division to the rise and fall of civilizations, each cycle fits into the larger rhythms of the earth and the cosmos.

Many ancient religions are based on these underlying cycles and rhythms of life. The fundamental cycle of birth, life, and death is symbolized in Hinduism by three primary gods who have equal power over the cosmos: Brahma the Creator, Vishnu the Preserver, and Shiva the Destroyer. Together they govern the interacting cycles of existence.

The *I Ching*, which forms the philosophical foundation of ancient Chinese thought, is based on the concept of a continuous cyclical fluctuation between two archetypical poles, known as yin and yang, the so-called feminine and masculine aspects of creation. The rhythmic interaction between what physicist Fritjov Capra called "the extreme poles of a single whole" underlies the fundamental movement of the universe.

Even today, cycles are an important aspect of our culture. Many of our holidays — like Christmas, Easter, Sukkot, and Thanksgiving — trace their origin to seasonal celebrations our ancestors created to commemorate the beginning of winter, the first breath of spring, or the autumn harvest. We celebrate birthdays and anniversaries, centenaries and millennia. Even when we say "Good morning" or "Good night," we acknowledge and celebrate the cyclic nature of each day. Although we are rarely aware of them, rhythms and cycles are intimately involved with literally every aspect of our lives in a multitude of ways.

The Rhythms of Self

Universal Intelligence is the wisdom that organizes the universe into all its rhythms, cycles, and patterns. This wisdom makes the rhythm of the helium atom different from the rhythm of the hydrogen atom, and makes the rhythm of flowing oil different from the rhythm of flowing water. Universal Intelligence also governs a rhythm of self. Its wisdom is found in our bodymind and guides us through our evolution on physical, emotional, mental, and spiritual levels.

Suffering occurs when the rhythm of our thoughts and actions is incompatible with the greater natural rhythms of our bodies and with the greater natural rhythms of life. When these rhythms cannot work in harmony for the growth and betterment of self, then suffering develops. Through suffering, we are able to experience an amplification of the rhythm of self and of the isolated, alienated, repressed, denied, or ignored rhythms of energy. Suffering is what makes us aware — even if not consciously — that our actions and thoughts are not in harmony with the greater rhythms that guide our lives.

By the time we arrive at Stage Two, we have healed enough to experience a duality between rhythms in a particular region of our body expressing their need for attention, and the rest of our body-mind. Any part of us that is ignored, denied, or alienated builds pressure or tension. As this polarized consciousness, region, energy pattern, or disassociated rhythm screams for its existence, it gains an unconscious control of more and more of our reality. It is often resentful, injured, distrustful, and foreign to our nature. Therefore, it is seen as "evil" or "wrong."

Our model of "evil things out there" is an important aspect of our medical systems, as illustrated by the "fight" against disease and the "magic bullets" to kill the evil bacteria or virus that is the cause of our trouble. Some people believe that their distress is caused by their asthma, arthritis, or cancer, but illness is a consequence of the body-mind striving for wholeness — it does not cause a lack of wholeness.

Our lack of wholeness is also projected into contemporary society. Bigotry, hatred, racism, and dogmatism are common in Stage Two, as are the fear of evil, "dark forces" and the devil, obsessive preoccupation with invaders from outer space, suspicion of foreigners, mistrust of different societies, and the attempt to categorize, separate, and control. In fact, many world problems are reflected in the early part of Stage Two. Solutions arise when we learn how to embrace the underlying rhythms of this important stage, on both an individual and a global scale.

Moving Through Stage Two

By the time we enter Stage Two, the dark, vast endlessness of suffering has been replaced by an awareness that the experiences we have been going through contain intervals that are free from suffering. Like other natural cycles and rhythms, suffering has a cycle or pattern of its own. We may find that our stomach cramps are more intense whenever we try to repress our anger, or that the suffering over the loss of our spouse is more intense when we go to bed at night or when we drive by a favorite restaurant on the way to work.

The lesson we learned from Stage One is, "Nothing is working right now. I am helpless." In contrast to Stage One, in Stage Two we have a glimpse of regaining our power even though it is through an external authority or mechanism. Instead of being totally engulfed by suffering, we see there is a pattern to what is — or is not — working; we become aware that there is a rhythm or cycle involved, and that we are involved in the process. And as we progress through Stage Two we ask ourselves, "What is the rhythm to this pattern?"

At the same time, our sense of self is strong enough to realize that we are now a "person suffering" rather than focusing only on the pain of the illness, the loss, or the divorce. In addition to an awareness of suffering as a cyclic pattern, there is a greater awareness that *I am the person* who is experiencing the suffering.

For example, Gilbert had a severe asthma attack one summer and thought he was going to die. He was rushed to the emergency room and was given medication and oxygen. He experienced the fear, discomfort, and helplessness that reflect the kind of suffering we described in Stage One. The following summer Gilbert had another asthma attack while on vacation, but the experience was different this time. He had the same degree of difficulty breathing, but did not feel as if he were going to die.

The quality of "something is seriously wrong" that appears in Stage One was not nearly as marked. Gilbert used his asthma medication and within minutes the "miracle" happened and he began breathing freely again. After the situation repeated itself over the next few months, Gilbert realized there was a pattern to his asthma. He did not know what it was or what to do about it, but he realized that something internal was going on, something that he was producing.

In the second stage of healing we often experience a sense of deja vu or memory of a previous event. Such memories are best left alone for now. This is not the time for probing as to why or how something happened. In Stage Two, what we experience is a process rather than an event. Analyzing the process only distracts us from our involvement, making us less able to feel our breath patterns, movements, and rhythms. As a result, we may throw ourselves into Stage One — Suffering — once more, or at least slow our movement through Stage Two. However, if we cannot resolve our connection with the rhythm of suffering and we move into Stage One again, this should not be interpreted as a sign of failure. There are times when repeated experiences are necessary to achieve deeper understanding and enrichment.

During the early stages of healing, when we look for the magical genie, we often ask for wishes that will satisfy our unresolved consciousness that is waiting to be set free. This consciousness is like an angry child who is throwing a temper tantrum because it isn't getting its needs met. Until we begin to acknowledge and understand this unresolved, polarized area of our being, the demands it will make — such as "An operation will solve this problem" or "A new car will make me happy" — will not bring about wholeness, enrichment, or healing. We are seeking to put an end to our suffering without creating the fundamental change in consciousness that is needed to bring about a major shift in our lives. As a result, we may ask for something that can create more problems than we had before.

Because other people, procedures, and things can never truly fill our emptiness, we will consistently sabotage our healing and move further away from the fulfillment we yearn for. However, as we move through subsequent stages of healing, our wishes will come from a more healed and integrated consciousness. Our consciousness will no longer be an isolated, angry child crying out for attention, but a more accepted aspect of our being that has much to teach us.

Toward the end of Stage Two, we become more aware of how judgment and polarities tend to manifest in our thoughts and conversations. We also begin to perceive how our actions can trigger certain responses in other people. Over time, we begin to see a dynamic of cause and effect in several areas of our lives and understand that we have a role in the process. At this point, we needn't figure out what our role is. We must only become aware that there is a rhythm or pattern to our suffering and that we participate in it. With this new awareness, we have embraced the central lesson of

Stage Two.

When we say "I have gone through this before," "It happened to me earlier in my life," "This feeling of being abused is familiar to me," or "My new husband reminds me so much of my ex," and we release this observation without analyzing it, we are ready to move on to Stage Three which teaches us that "I am stuck in a perspective."

Therapeutic Involvement

I mentioned that, for those who are in Stage Two, modern medicine is often very effective. It provides us with prognoses that are often not very favorable and acknowledges that we are victims of forces beyond our control. It also provides the opportunity for the practitioner or treatment to become a hero or savior, which is important to us in this stage of our healing. This is why most people involved in the early part of Stage Two are not very open to alternative medicine or holistic methods which primarily foster self-healing and personal responsibility.

At this point in the healing process, we would rather identify with an authority figure as a higher power who has the responsibility to control or govern our lives. To have the practitioner act as a friend or helper can actually disempower us at this point in the healing process. In the latter part of Stage Two, we may be more open to holistic and alternative healing, with the practitioner serving more as a helper than as a savior.

If you, the practitioner, are aware of this dynamic, you can anticipate the problem. When you see patients in the early part of Stage Two, when judgment occurs, the best approach may be to say, "Yes, I can help you. I can help save you from your distress for a period of time. I will play that role only for a short period, until your body can figure out how to do it on its own." By stating that you are primarily a bridge between levels of consciousness, you help your patients see their situations in more expanded perspectives. They can readily accept your healing message because the truth of this statement resonates with them. You are still a genie, but a genie who facilitates the potential for personal transformation rather than being the transformation itself.

Although Stage Two involves an awareness of suffering as part of a pattern or process, asking patients to figure out what the pattern is can often intensify the suffering of early Stage Two or throw them into Stage One once more. At this time, their bodymind has not evolved enough to embrace healing or wholeness in order to understand or remedy the pattern.

Hearing Yourself Ask for Help

Asking or praying for help in Stage Two may sound like, "Oh, God, please make this chemotherapy work" or "God, please make this investment change everything." Conversations will often revolve around your expectations of how the new method, procedure, or person will change everything for you.

Stage Two Exercises

Stage Two exercises enable us to experience the separate rhythms in our bodies. They also invite these rhythms to join the wholeness of our larger rhythms.

The breathing pattern is the same as in Stage One: breathe in through your nose and out through your mouth. Rather than laying both hands simultaneously on the same spot at each of three regions, place both hands on different regions at the same time. Place one hand on your upper chest and the other hand on your navel. Breathe, connecting your breath to the movement under your top hand; then breathe connecting your breath to the movement under your bottom hand.

Move your hands down so your top hand is lying at the bottom of your breastbone and your other hand is on your abdomen. Repeat the alternate breathing. Direct your breath into the region of your body you are touching. In each case feel the difference in the rhythms or the rate and style of the body rising and falling under your hands.

Finally, place one hand on top of your chest and the other hand over the navel region. Repeat the breathing again, feeling the connection of the rhythms through the distance between both hands. You may experience difficulty in feeling the rhythm between two areas. If so, move your hands to the two areas where you can get a sense of the rhythm. As you breathe, slowly increase the distance between your hands. Eventually sense the rhythm under one hand communicating or meeting the rhythm of the other hand.

If you feel that it is difficult to put your hand on one part of your body and breathe into that area, use the Stage One exercises rather than those of Stage Two. When you complete the Stage One exercises, return to the Stage Two exercises. Note when you feel a difference between the body's movements under each hand. Remark "I have different rhythms, different parts."

Stage Two Declarations

When the breathing exercise is almost complete, make the following declarations to affirm your movement with Stage Two:

"I have polarities, rhythms and differences within me."

"I have parts that have not talked with each other for some time."

That is the extent of the understanding necessary in this second stage of healing.

Stage Two Exercise

3

STAGE THREE

Stuck in a Perspective

*He who cannot change the very fabric of his thought
will never be able to change reality and will never,
therefore, make any progress.* — ANWAR SADAT

Have you ever reached a point in a relationship when you felt that it wasn't going anywhere? When you and your partner were arguing about the same old issues, yet nothing ever changed?

Have you ever come to the realization that you were in a dead-end job? Although at first you liked the job, you became bored with the same procedures and had nothing new to look forward to.

Perhaps you have been complaining about an ankle you injured in an automobile accident ten years ago, or you suffered a heart attack years ago that still restricts your enjoyment of life. Maybe you have the same infection in your right ear for the fourth time this year.

As we enter Stage Three, we still feel that the old injury, disease, or trauma is the cause of our current problems. Often, we will experience an uneasy feeling that "my body (or mind) is holding onto something" or "I want to move ahead, but I can't." In other words, we realize we are stuck in an old way of seeing things — we are stuck in a perspective. This realization may occur gradually or suddenly. Like Sleeping Beauty, who is awakened with a kiss, we may suddenly awake from the slumber of not being aware of the deeper realities involved with the source of our distress. In a sense, we are awakened by the kiss of truth.

In this stage of healing, we recognize that the pattern — or process — we observed in Stage Two is somehow connected to how we perceive life, adapt to life, and recover from life's events. The shift from Stage Two to Stage Three is remarkable because we develop a stronger sense of self along with the strength that allows us to assume a greater degree of responsibility toward our situation.

Joe's Story

Joe and Cynthia had been married for three years when Cynthia mentioned that she wanted to have a child. Joe reluctantly agreed, and Cynthia soon became pregnant. Cynthia was ecstatic about becoming a mother, and Joe apparently shared her happiness. Yet, shortly after hearing the news of her pregnancy, Joe had an affair with a co-worker named Janice. After Cynthia found out, she filed for divorce.

Joe's relationship with Janice continued for two years and was slowly becoming more intimate. When Janice's brother was diagnosed with cancer, she began to rely on Joe for emotional support. After her brother died, Janice brought up the possibility of their living together. Although Joe outwardly agreed that it was a good idea, within a week he told her that he no longer found her attractive, and within a month they split up.

Joe's life was becoming more difficult. Finances were tight and he was close to filing for bankruptcy. Although he regretted the breakup of his two previous relationships, Joe believed that his suffering was due to the women in his life and the torment of his financial problems.

Joe began taking courses in money management and learned how to improve his methods of doing business. His financial condition improved, and his professional life moved forward again, but his thoughts often returned to his failed relationships. He couldn't quite put his finger on the cause of their failure and he felt uneasy about them.

One day Joe was having dinner with Patricia, a woman he had been dating for several months. She talked to him about their relationship and shared with him her desire for a greater level of commitment and intimacy. As she spoke, Joe began to experience a familiar uneasiness. "Where did this come from?" Joe asked himself.

Suddenly, Joe became lost in a timeless void where emotions, thoughts, and connections come together in a flash, as if a portal of consciousness opened within his mind. He saw the link between Cynthia's wish to have children, Janice's wanting to move in with him, and Patricia's desire for commitment. He also realized that he was stuck: he wasn't emotionally available for any of them.

Joe had just moved through the second stage of healing (observing that there was a pattern to his suffering) and then into the third stage, in which he realized that he was stuck in a perspective. He still did not know exactly what the perspective was, but he knew he was stuck. He simply realized that every time he attained a certain level of intimacy in his relationships, he suddenly left his partner. This realization changed his life.

Like Joe, when we realize that we are stuck in a perspective, we also realize that we are responsible for the result.

New Bodymind, Old Patterns

The body we have at this moment is not the same body we had five years ago, five months ago, or even five days ago. Every cell in our body is in the process of dying and being replaced by new cells. This process continues throughout our lifetime, with different body cells being renewed and replaced at different rates. According to Deepak Chopra, M.D.,

> Ninety-eight percent of the atoms in your body were not there a year ago. The skeleton that seems so solid was not there a year ago. . . . The skin is new every month. You have a new stomach lining every four days, with the actual surface cells that contact food being renewed

every five minutes. The cells in the liver turn over very
slowly, but new atoms still flow through them, like water
in a river course, making a new liver every six weeks.

In a sense, our shoulders, hearts, and stomachs are brand new.
Within a twenty-year period, our vertebrae have been replaced at
least ten times, while the softer muscle tissue that surrounds them
has been replaced many dozens of times.

If this is true, why do we have the same back problem, heart
problem, or relationship pattern throughout much of our lives? The
answer lies in the nervous system. As opposed to the organs, soft tissues, and bony structures of the body that are constantly regenerat-
ing, nerve cells do not regenerate. And it is the nervous system that
coordinates the consciousness of all body parts, systems, functions,
and patterns.

The Nervous System: Our Healing Foundation

The nervous system is constantly at work. It receives, processes,
and transmits messages to and from every part of our body to help
us respond to, adapt to, recover from, and experience our environment. If we touch a hot skillet, our nervous system will tell us — in
a fraction of a second and in no uncertain terms — that the extreme
heat is dangerous and we should remove our hand.

The nervous system maintains our body's inner environment and
regulates the digestion of food and the amount of carbon dioxide in
our blood without our awareness. Whether we move our eyes across
a page to read these words or secrete intestinal fluids to digest the
salad we had for lunch, our nervous system is involved and performs
its tasks with precision and lightning speed.

By acting as a conduit for the expression of Universal Consciousness (our innate wisdom), the nervous system establishes who
we are and how we deal with the world. What our body feels — not
necessarily what we are consciously aware of — actually changes
the way we perceive the world. If the nervous system is stuck in one

perspective, the messages it will send and receive will be stuck in that perspective as well. In other words, when the nervous system has not been able to recover from the trauma of past events — whether physical, emotional, or chemical — our emotional reality is also stuck.

Spinal Tension and Nerve Interference

Health, well-being, vitality, and wholeness are functions of a nervous system that is free from interference. Factors that produce interference include medications, alcohol, environmental pollutants, and chemicals in the food supply. Electromagnetic radiation from electrical appliances, computer screens, power lines, aircraft, cellular telephones, and electric blankets can also create interference. Physical pressure exerted on the nervous system from bones, tumors, wounds, or other sources of mechanical tension — pulling, stretching, squeezing, or twisting of the delicate nervous system — also produces consistent alterations in function and inhibits the body's ability to heal.

The combined effect of various stresses and the inability of the nervous system to deal with them produces a subluxation (interference) of the spine. A structural subluxation occurs when the spinal bones become stuck from moving within their normal range of movement. This is usually the result of a mechanical or physical stress from which the body has not recovered. A facilitated subluxation occurs when the nervous system has not reset itself from predominantly emotional, mental, or chemical stress.

When the spine is stuck in a limited range of motion, it often produces a nervous system that is much less able to recover from life's stresses. This interference disrupts the nervous system's natural ability to assemble and sort out neurological instructions. Like a computer, if the input (messages to the system) is distorted in any way, then the output (messages from the nervous system to each body cell) will also be distorted. Emotional traumas, accidents, or breathing polluted air are challenges to a compromised nervous system.

The ability of the bodymind to "reset" itself is greatly hindered.

Stuck in the Body; Stuck in the Mind

The body and the mind are one unit; it is impossible to be stuck in the body without being stuck in the mind. This observation is well known to bodyworkers like John C. Pierrakos, M.D., a psychiatrist and developer of Core Energetic Therapy:

> The constrictions of energy . . . are not isolated dysfunctions. They are blocks of stultified energy that trammel the physical body in skeletomuscular rigidities, and also disrupt the higher planes of energy, thus affecting mental attitudes.

The mental and emotional dynamic that results from this situation is clearly described by the well-known counselor, Dr. John Bradshaw, in his book *Bradshaw On: The Family:*

> This frozen pattern clogs one's creative intelligence. It forms a trigger which functions like the "on" button of a tape recorder. Whenever any new or similar experience happens, the old recording starts to play. Here we see the force and power of behavioral conditioning. Like Pavlov's dog, whenever stimulation occurs, the response automatically takes place. This is the basis for re-actions or re-enactments. The past so contaminates the intelligence, that the new and creative responses are not possible.

In my practice I found that the shape, position, tone, and tension of the spinal system is directly related to the shape, position, tone, and tension in a person's life. It makes sense that when the spine loses its flexibility and natural contours, so does a person's life experiences. With a spine that is less flexible and does not recover from its experiences, the person will most likely be stuck in a perspective. This becomes especially relevant when we look at the relationship among the vertebrae, their associated nerves, and related organs.

In addition, with each position of the spine, there is a corresponding predisposition of consciousness, mood, or personality. For example, when a person's back and head bend downward, we associate that position with defeat or depression; a spine that is ramrod straight with the head pulled back is a sign of emotional and mental rigidity. When the spine cannot enjoy its natural, full range of motion, the bodymind is limited in the kinds of experiences it can have, as well as in the ways it can express itself on physical, mental, emotional, and spiritual levels. The bodymind will be predisposed to certain kinds of experiences while being unable to respond to others.

This mechanism may be why reoccurring pain is often on the same side of the body or affects the same organ. When we experience the same periodic back pain, the same intestinal cramps, or the same asthma flares, we need to consider the possibility that our bodymind is stuck in a perspective. Being stuck rarely has anything to do with a conscious choice to be that way. It is more a consequence of a fixated nervous system due to a spinal distortion or related problem.

Ron's Story

Ron had been a friend of my wife's family since high school. At thirty years of age, he was strong and handsome. He was everyone's friend and was always willing to do things for others. If your car broke down, he would stop what he was doing and fix it. If you needed money, he was glad to help out. Happily married, he had a twelve-year-old son, who was the image of himself, and a nine-year-old daughter.

One afternoon my wife learned that Ron had just returned from the hospital. He had been diagnosed with metastatic lung cancer that had spread to the bowel. He had undergone both surgery and radiation therapy. His case was pronounced terminal, and he was sent home to spend his final days with his family.

Ron's wife asked me to attend to him as a chiropractor — not to treat his cancer — in the hope that I could help free interference in his spinal system and empower his self-healing system.

It was a shock to see him. He was lying in a hospital bed that was set up in the living room. His head was bald and his body emaciated. Part of his intestines had been removed in the treatment of the bowel cancer. Ron's breathing was shallow and his eyes were glassy. He was not very responsive to conversation. His legs had become paralyzed during his stay in the hospital and were propped up on pillows. Ron knew that his case was hopeless and that he was going to die.

Gathering my inner composure, I began by saying, "I cannot cure what is wrong with you, nor can I do anything for your distress." I told him that as a chiropractor I could only help free up that which was perfect within him — the coordinating intelligence of the body — by correcting interferences in his central nervous system at the spinal level. All the corrections I made involved very gentle contacts to his spine. I told him that I did not know if the cancer would go away or whether he would die. He looked at me. I added that part of him was trying to die, which was obvious. The more important question was, which parts of him wanted to live?

When a person has experienced a marked emotional or physical trauma, certain parts of the spinal musculature will have a characteristic "thickness" from years of tension and contractions. If we experience the loss of a loved one, for example, our spinal musculature will tense. It is natural for our body to respond this way, but sometimes our nervous system becomes stuck (does not recover from the trauma because of an interference in its ability to be flexible). The muscle pattern or tension persists because the nervous system continues to experience the trauma as if it were still happening.

This response is most often unconscious.

Our body movement and tension reveal the history of our phys-iology whether or not we are consciously aware of it. After study-ing the case histories of hundreds of people, I found that if some-one had surgery, and if an accident had also taken place at about the same time, often a related emotional trauma happened as well, because the body and the mind do not attract traumas separately. Physical traumas are sometimes the only way a person will experi-ence feelings.

With this in mind, let us return to Ron. When I checked his spine, his musculature indicated that at about the age of twelve he had suf-fered a severe emotional trauma and his bodymind was acting as if the trauma were still taking place.

I asked Ron what had happened when he was twelve. His par-ents were in the room, and when he didn't respond his mother said, "Well, he broke his hip that year." That was indeed a physical trau-ma, but his spinal posture indicated there also had been an emo-tional trauma. When I asked if anything else had happened, his mother replied that Ron also had his appendix removed the same year.

Then his father mentioned that Ron almost lost both his legs the following year because of a bone infection. Ron's history was becoming more clear to me: here was a boy who broke his hip in a bicycle accident, had an emergency appendectomy, and nearly lost both legs, all at about the same time. It appeared that some kind of pattern involving his lower body was repeating itself.

I then asked, "What emotional loss may have taken place?" For the first time in his adult life, Ron began to cry, as he nodded yes. His mother said that at age twelve, Ron witnessed the violent death of one of his closest friends. Nothing more was said.

I continued to examine Ron's spine and located the subluxation that inhibited the function of his innate intelligence. I then applied a gentle touch to several vertebrae and within minutes Ron raised himself and smiled. His nervous system was slowly being freed from the perspective it was stuck in.

When I saw Ron three days later, his wife said that he had revealed something he had never told anyone. When he was twelve years old, he challenged his best friend to catch a ride on the side of a moving bus. When his friend refused, Ron teased him and called him names until he agreed to do it. After barely grabbing onto the side of the bus, his friend lost his grip, fell under the bus, was run over by the wheels, and killed instantly. Ron watched in horror as his friend's legs and abdomen were crushed by the vehicle. He never told anyone that he felt responsible for his friend's death.

Several days after Ron told this story, he started gaining weight and began moving around the house and yard. He became more open with others, and he and his family began to have the most meaningful dialogues of their lives. Music and laughter were heard in the house once more. As Ron continued receiving regular spinal adjustments, I no longer saw a man who was dying, but someone who was reclaiming his life. Over the next few weeks, the quality of his life dramatically improved.

One night an associate of mine visited Ron to adjust his spine and Ron told her that he couldn't fight the cancer anymore and that he had decided to "move on." He couldn't remain stuck any longer. The following day Ron called his wife and children together and said that he was "going home." They held his hand while he described his ascension process as going through a door of light. Within a few minutes he was gone.

Ron's nervous system had been stuck in an emotional perspective that produced a physical reality. He realized that he no longer wanted to be stuck in that perspective, but his adherence to it did not allow him to move back toward suffering again.

I am not a psychologist, but I am aware of people's responses to the healing process. There is certainly a relationship between unacknowledged consciousness and expression of disease. Somehow, the consciousness we are blocked from "being with" will find a physical or emotional way to be with us. This is not to say that a particular disease is the result of a specific kind of physical or emotional trauma. But what is important is to realize that being stuck in the perspective of a particular trauma can have physiological consequences and cumulative effects years later. As with Ron's case, the physical or emotional symptoms appear to be directly related to an earlier unresolved trauma.

Sarah's Stage Three Experience

In Chapter Two we discussed Sarah, who realized there was a pattern to her heart condition. Sarah moved from Stage Two to Stage Three while still in the hospital. As she lay in bed and looked back on her life, she felt as though a light bulb went on above her head. She suddenly realized that her belief that a high protein diet rich in animal fat was necessary for good health, as well as her belief that "fat middle-aged matrons like myself don't need to go jogging around the running track," had something to do with her heart problem. She later said, "I realized that I was sitting on a train heading straight for a heart attack, and that my old ways of thinking about diet and exercise had put me on that train." Sarah's perspectives were not necessarily emotional; she realized that she was simply stuck in an old way of seeing things.

Arthur's Story

Arthur came to my office one night with his body bent to one side. He was in great pain. His fists were clenched, and he needed a cane for support. He had difficulty getting around, and sitting was impossible.

Arthur was a captain of an excursion boat. As he was bending over to make a repair, he felt a snap in his back and then experienced extreme pain. He had consulted an orthopedic physician who treated his pain, but it had not gone away. Arthur's family convinced him that he needed healing rather than curing. Although very skeptical, Arthur came to me.

I began by telling him that I understood he was in a lot of pain, but I could do nothing for it, nor would I attempt to. I told him that if he would like his nervous system to function more effectively, I could assist him by adjusting his spine. I added that I did not know whether the adjustment would increase or decrease his pain, nor could I assure him that he wouldn't feel additional pain in areas he didn't know about yet. I told him, "You can't heal it until you can feel it."

Out of deference to his family, Arthur decided to let me adjust his spine. I examined it, and because of the tense feel of the musculature, asked him if an emotional trauma occurred about twenty years earlier. His case history had revealed no major trauma. He replied that nothing had happened, but added that his brother died in Vietnam twenty-three years ago. He added that this issue shouldn't have anything to do with his back now, because he just hurt it while making a repair.

When I found where the interference needed to be addressed, I carefully adjusted the spine in the area where his neck met his skull. The results were dramatic. Within seconds Arthur's spinal posture began to shift; his neck was no longer pitched forward, and his fists were no longer clenched. He placed his cane on the floor and sat up comfortably. He said, "You know, I almost cried today from the pain. I never cry. I never even cried when my brother died." I had not asked him for that revelation, nor did I expect him to say anything of that nature. Yet his comment is characteristic of what happens when a nervous system is freed from a perspective. The interference blocking the nervous system from moving into the next level of reality is discharged. It is not unlike driving for hours and suddenly realizing that our vision has been impaired by a buildup of mud on the windshield.

As we sat for a few minutes listening to a rendition of Pachelbel's "Canon" that included sounds of the ocean and birds, Arthur suddenly started to cry. He told me how he hated birds because they annoyed him so much while he worked. Now he realized that they were God's voice speaking, a comment coming from a person who had no interest or training in spiritual matters. As I left him to attend to other patients, he said, "I just want to get lost in the sounds of the tape."

The second time I saw Arthur, I adjusted another vertebra in his neck, and he reexperienced a trauma to the point that he thought blood was coming out of his mouth. He began punching the air and screaming, "It's broken! It's broken!" while holding onto his jaw and face. He was re-living an event that took place about three years after his brother had died. One day his father had lost his temper and had tried to kill Arthur by pushing a refrigerator on top of him. He not only reexperienced the facial distortion of that one-time impact, but he reexperienced the trauma, the emotions, and the unresolved information he needed to go through. His reactions were not expected, nor were they solicited. They came up when his nervous system became freed from a perspective.

When Arthur finally stood up, he said, "The pain is gone," but his anger toward his father surfaced once more. He suddenly stooped over again in pain. Without a word, he immediately saw the relationship between the rage toward his father, his spinal distortion, and his pain.

Within a short time Arthur began moving with more freedom than he had felt in years. He also experienced a peace of mind he had not previously experienced. One day after an adjustment he told me, "I will not take this anymore. I won't let this happen to me again. I deserve more than this." As we will see later, this kind of statement is typical of the movement from Stage Three to Stage Four.

Moving Through Stage Three

Stage Three is very powerful because it serves as a bridge between being in suffering and doing something about it. By the time people reach this stage of healing, they have probably tried physical interventions (drugs, surgery, or physical therapy) or psychological analysis or psychotherapy. But the practitioner who was once the "savior" is no longer as helpful.

Often people entering Stage Three are dissatisfied with the care they are receiving because it addresses the problem as though it were a chronic or permanent state of being. As a result, treatment is based on a particular condition, and patients continue to receive the same treatment for extended periods of time. In other words, patients are stuck in a perspective, and the treatment used to deal with the problem is stuck in a perspective as well.

In Stage Three, one factor that inhibits healing is the naming of a condition. Although identifying the problem ("You have arthritis") may bring peace of mind, the same mindset can prevent us from seeing beyond the symptom. For example, Dorothy came to me suffering from arthritis. She had trouble opening and closing her hands because it was painful to do so. Dorothy was given a medical diagnosis when she was in Stage Two, and the perspective she had was that she couldn't move her hands because she had arthritis and that arthritis was the cause of her pain.

In reality, arthritis is a name given to a set of symptoms that include the fact that hands cannot open easily and that some joint degeneration is taking place. When I discussed this concept with Dorothy, she was not able to understand the point I was trying to make: The arthritis did not make her sick. The sickness came about because she was not flexible enough and not adaptable enough. Perhaps she was not aware of the emotional factor or other factors that may have been behind the pattern that promoted her condition.

As we move through Stage Three, naming symptoms or labeling conditions can distract us from the healing process unless we simply move with the rhythm of the statement "I am (or have been) stuck in a perspective." Later, when the time is right, our bodymind will reveal the underlying reasons to our conscious mind.

Some people remain in Stage Three for a long time. They speak about how their old heart attacks or bad backs still affect them today, but they move no further. Others stay stuck in a relationship or a job they don't like for many years. They realize they are stuck, yet do not feel they have options to enable them to move forward.

I have found that the more flexible and adaptable the nervous system, the easier it is for the individual to move through Stage Three. Individuals who are body, movement, or breath centered — like athletes, dancers, and those involved in yoga, stretching, hiking, aerobics, and other forms of exercise — move through Stage Three with minimum intervention. This is because they are more aware of what it is like not to reach the peak performance they are accustomed to.

On the other hand, people who are not physically active or who have not experienced peak physical performance are often not aware of the full range of motion their joints could go through, so they don't feel they are missing anything. To quote Alexander Lowen, M.D., the developer of bioenergetics,

> The person who is out of touch with his body doesn't know that he is closed off. He will talk of love, he will even make some gestures of love, but since his heart isn't in either his words or his actions, they will fail to be convincing.

People who consistently experience muscular aches and pains, sore and stiff joints, backaches, and neck pain often have difficulty moving through this stage, because the awareness of being stuck takes place only as the "stuckedness" starts releasing.

Flowing With Stage Three

At the beginning of Stage Three, we realize that we are stuck in a perspective, but often we still don't know what the perspective is. We may try to figure out why we are stuck, but as with earlier stages, trying to figure it out often leads us out of the rhythm and produces more distress. It becomes a distraction from the process we are involved with at this moment. Analyzing our problem or thinking about it can also intensify the pattern and produce more distress or suffering because "where one's attention goes, the energy flows."

While thinking or talking about the problem does not resolve it, feeling it can. In *Depression and the Body*, Dr. Lowen wrote,

> The patient must be brought into touch with reality — the reality of his life situation, the reality of his feelings, and the reality of his body. These three realities cannot be separated from one another. The person who is in touch with his feelings is also in touch with his body and life situation. By the same logic, the person who is in touch with his body is in touch with all aspects of his reality.

As we surrender to the dynamics of this important stage, as opposed to trying to figure out why we are stuck, we automatically get in touch with the natural rhythm of our bodymind and feel the region of stuckedness as though it were a large rock blocking the flow of a stream. As we honor our healing process, conscious awareness occurs at the proper time, rather than occurring because of analysis, concentration, or control.

As with the other stages of healing, the time it takes to move through Stage Three is unique to each individual. One person can remain in Stage Three for several years or may move back and forth between stages One, Two, and Three repeatedly until sufficient integration has taken place and the pattern is somehow resolved. Another may move through Stage Three in a matter of minutes. Whatever the time period may be, the point to understand is that surrendering to the consciousness of Stage Three is essential for moving through it and onward to subsequent stages of healing.

Seeking Help

During stages One and Two, we often seek practitioners who can control the chaos and restore order in our life. In Stage Three, we begin to recognize that it is the control of the chaos which creates a limited perspective physically, emotionally, mentally, and spiritually. And this contributes to, and perpetuates, our suffering. For people who realize they are stuck in a perspective, Stage Three offers a perfect opportunity to seek the assistance of holistic practitioners whose goal is to facilitate the healing process rather than to control symptoms.

Those who work to release energetic blocks, improve body flexibility, and remove the causes of nerve interference are particularly beneficial at this stage. Massage therapists, craniosacral therapists, acupuncturists, shiatsu practitioners, non-therapeutic chiropractors, and Therapeutic Touch and Zero Balancing practitioners are some of the best. Healing disciplines like Jungian therapy, neo-Reichian therapy, bioenergetics, Core Energetic Therapy, Hellerwork, and Pre-Cognitive Re-education can also provide large windows of entry, so to speak, for individuals to move through Stage Three and beyond.

Assessment Questions for Stage Three

Have I seen this pattern before?

Do I feel my body is locked (arms, shoulders, back)?

Do I feel tension in my muscles?

When the pattern comes up, am I aware of a certain tightening in my arms, chest, or neck?

Does my breathing become shallower and more restricted when the pattern comes up?

When I feel this pattern, do I experience internal agitation? Is there upset, anger? Is there an emotional charge?

Do I continue recreating situations I don't want, don't like, or resent?

Hearing Yourself Ask for Help

When you ask for help in Stage Three, it will mostly sound like, "Please help me get unstuck. I must move on."

Stage Three Exercise

Sit, or lie comfortably on your back. Place one hand on top of the other and lay them just below your neck. Breathe easily and deeply in through your nose and out through your mouth.

Move your hands slightly to your heart, and continue breathing for another minute or so. Continue moving your hands downward to different areas of your body. Use the declarations below and pay careful attention to any region that is tense or disturbed. As you reach this area, place your hands over it and gently breathe into it. Do not try to free the area or change it in any way. Just be OK with the stage you are in, and acknowledge your stuckedness with a gentle nod of your head, and then move on to the next region which may feel blocked or stuck. You may twist your body or squirm into a position which increases your experience of the blockage while you hold your hands over the involved area.

Stage Three Declarations

Please state in order as your experience the blocked area.

"I am stuck right here." (As you move your hand gently over the stuck region.)

"I acknowledge this region."

"I am sorry I haven't noticed you before in a more loving way."

Stage Three Exercise

4

STAGE FOUR

Reclaiming Our Power

I take my power back. I honor my inner being.
I reclaim my wholeness.

Stage Four is a major doorway to reclaiming our personal power and affirming responsibility for our healing.

The statement that best expresses this stage is, "I'm not going to take this anymore!" At the beginning of Stage Four, this statement is often preceded by "I'm mad as hell . . ." made famous by the movie *Network*. It reflects the realization that our suffering — be it physical, emotional, or economic — is the result of our lack of wholeness. We have been disconnected from our inner essence, and we no longer wish to remain this way.

The key phrases that often come to mind in Stage Four are dynamic and direct:

"I want my power back."
"I deserve more than this."
"I cannot keep giving my power away."
"I have to stop selling myself short."
"This can't go on."
"I must honor who I really am."
"I am not going to take this anymore."

The fourth stage of healing resonates with the fairy tale "The Frog Prince." In this story, a frog fetches a golden ball that has fallen into a well for a beautiful princess. In return, the princess promises to love him, have him as her companion, let him eat from her plate, and sleep in her bed. Yet, when he visits the castle to ask that she stand by her promise, she refuses, only to be ordered by her father, "That which you have promised, in thy time of necessity, you must perform." Eventually, in a fit of rage, the princess picks up the frog and throws it against the wall, which releases a spell and turns the frog into a handsome prince. They soon marry and live happily ever after.

In Stage Four, it is as though we are the princess and have a promise to fulfill to those aspects of ourselves we have dishonored (the frog) that are demanding our attention and intimacy. In this stage we obey the calling of our higher self (the king) to make good on our promises, which the alienated and hidden parts of our nature demand of us. When we reach our true feelings (when the princess throws the frog against the wall), the spell is broken and transformation takes place.

The Bifurcation Point

Stage Four is one of the more interesting stages of healing, because it offers a variety of challenges that can divert us from healing. At the beginning of this stage, we again arrive at an important bifurcation point; we reach a fork in the road in our healing journey and can choose one of two paths. The path we choose will determine the direction of our healing process.

As we enter the first path — the one most commonly chosen — we say, "I've had it! No more!" We separate ourselves from our suffering by actively rejecting our symptoms, our pain, or the apparent source of our suffering. We may leave a relationship, undergo surgery, quit our job, or put the house up for sale. We want to do everything possible to remove ourselves from our distress, and Stage Four provides the opportunity.

The other path — the one less often chosen — involves a different state of awareness. Although we may still say to ourselves "No more!", this statement is often followed by, "I cannot continue getting myself into these situations." Rather than wanting to separate from the apparent external cause of our suffering (such as the difficult relationship or the painful back), we assume a greater degree of responsibility for the deeper, less obvious factors that may underlie our situation.

Stage Four represents a dynamic phase in the healing process. We have now achieved a sense of self strong enough to realize that we have dishonored our inner essence (which we may call the God within, innate wisdom, our higher self, or our inner healer). In this stage we decide to turn our backs on our suffering and move in a new direction.

To illustrate, let us return to Joe, whose story we described in the previous chapter. While having dinner with his girlfriend, Joe felt the urge to leave her, as he had done with his two previous partners. In Stage Two, Joe realized there was a pattern involved in his suffering; in Stage Three, he realized that he was stuck in a perspective which caused him to leave his relationships whenever they became too intimate.

In the fourth stage of healing, the most common reaction would be for Joe to say, "I've had it with these dependent women! I'm out of here!" Although this choice will resolve his immediate situation, it will not result in healing. But, if Joe chooses the other path, he may say to himself, "This scenario I've created is so painful. It has to stop." With this statement, Joe shifts the focus from his girlfriends to himself and begins to take greater responsibility for his situation. At the same time, he declares his desire to liberate himself from his old perspective, thus reclaiming his power. This is the essence of Stage Four.

By choosing the first path, Joe makes a decision he hopes will resolve his situation. But, by choosing the second path, Joe doesn't have to make a decision about leaving the relationship at all. All he has to do is realize that he wants to let go of the old perspective. He is not yet consciously aware that he is afraid of intimacy and commitment. He just knows that he wants something more. There is no other choice to be made at this stage. By saying "I will not take this anymore," Joe becomes aware there is a pattern going on. And his sense of self is strong enough for him to realize that this pattern may be distorted.

If Joe chooses the first path, he will either stay out of relationships for awhile or become involved with someone else and repeat the pattern. This, in fact, is what most of us do. Relationships tend to bring about our greatest challenges because we often attract partners who express the alienated aspects of ourselves. In an intimate relationship, whatever we repress, our partners will often express. Within the relationship of the bodymind, repressed information will be expressed in another area of the body or in another aspect of our lives, such as work, finances, or relationships.

Seeing the discomfort, the pain, and the patterns as aspects of life from which we need to separate ourselves is totally different from seeing those patterns and experiences as *expressions of disconnection*, or rhythms that are not in tune with the larger rhythms of our life. It is as though life were an orchestra playing a symphony, with one musician insisting on playing a song — no matter how beautiful it may be — that is out of tune or rhythm with the rest of the orchestra.

Finding Order in Chaos

Stage Four is not a time to decide what to do, but is rather the stage of reclaiming our power. This is perhaps the most common stage when we seek holistic practitioners whose goal is to foster self-empowerment. As we receive the care needed to remove interference from our internal communications system, we become more in touch with our inherent natural rhythms. As a result, we become more aware of ourselves and have a clearer idea about what the next step of our healing journey will consist of.

When we begin to move through Stage Four, we do not need to

know that we are becoming empowered. If we say, "I have to change, but I don't know what to do," we can be assured that the time to change has not yet arrived. When changes are necessary, our internal wisdom will tell us exactly what we need. If we are not sure whether we need to change, it may be that our bodymind has not yet healed enough to accommodate that change. Change becomes effortless at the appropriate stage in our healing.

Many people do not complete Stage Four. Although it offers major opportunities for growth and healing, it is also full of pitfalls that can distract or deter us from the healing process. Stage Four is similar to the description of the spiritual journey described by Roberto Assagioli:

> Man's spiritual development is a long and arduous journey, an adventure through strange lands full of surprises, difficulties and even dangers. It involves a drastic transformation of the "normal" elements of the personality, an awakening of the potentialities hitherto dormant, a raising of consciousness to new realms, and a functioning along a new inner dimension.

This is the stage in which, for example, people no longer want the discomfort in the relationship or the insecurity of the financial disturbance. As a result, many will produce new patterns in an attempt to control this chaos. "Easy" ways out include finding other partners, avoiding relationships altogether, changing jobs, or relocating. Others will seek therapeutic intervention from a medical doctor, symptom-oriented chiropractor, osteopath, physical therapist, psychotherapist or financial counselor to regain control or order in their lives.

If these efforts are reactions to the "I'm mad as hell and I'm not going to take this anymore" mindset, then often these reactions produce more chaos than they were intended to control. However, the same decisions made later in Stage Four take on a totally different meaning and support wholeness, because those decisions are no longer reactions to the upset of previous powerlessness, but are actions born from the commitment for wholeness. The lesson that is contained in this stage of healing — honoring one's essence — involves a constant enfolding and unfolding between chaos and order.

Physicists have discovered that chaos is an essential part of daily existence and is necessary for life. They have also found that, ironically, chaos also contains a sense of order that lies beyond appearances. As Anna Lemkow observed in *The Wholeness Principle*,

> Chaos science finds that irregularities . . . are not devoid of order, that even seemingly chaotic processes such as weather patterns and turbulence in fluids are found, on detailed analysis, to exhibit subtle strands of order.

Rather than repressing the chaos in our lives, we need to experience its energy, learn what it may have to teach us, and discover the underlying order behind its appearance. Since chaos governs our nervous system, our ability to create order out of chaos is a sign of growth and development.

Procedures as Distractions

In Stage Four we are often tempted to add more structure and procedure to our lives in an attempt to gain a greater degree of control. However, by following procedures, we do not get in touch with the underlying adverse tension in our spines, bodies, or lives. We can actually keep ourselves from participating in the healing process by remaining too busy to feel the underlying issues. Unlike Stage Two, when the procedures are glorified as the magical genie, procedures undertaken in Stage Four keep us busy, occupied, or distracted from our awareness.

Decisions often made in the earlier part of Stage Four are reactions to our frustrations ("I'm mad as hell . . ."), which usually lead us to make choices from our separateness (Stage Two). These decisions include going on diets, getting other jobs, meeting new people, learning new techniques or trying other therapies, all done with the intent of reclaiming the power outside ourselves. As mentioned earlier, however, the later part of Stage Four does not involve making choices, but simply the decision to honor one's self.

I am not suggesting that exercise programs, educational seminars, new methodologies, healthier diets, or new friends are not effective. Choices such as these may be effective when we have moved into Stage Six. But the decisions to change our lives that we make in Stage Four can divert us from the healing journey if we have not yet developed the flexibility, perspective, or level of consciousness to make decisions that will be best for us in the long term.

In Stage Four, we need to simply say, "I won't take this anymore. I want to take my power back." "I will separate myself from any situation that does not let me express my power. I am greater than I am allowing myself to be." That is the furthest we need to go in Stage Four.

If you declare "I am not going to take this anymore," you are not saying "I am going to sell my business" or "I am going to get involved in a new relationship." Such steps are not taken until you have reached a level of flexibility and your bodymind has evolved to the point that you are more consistent with your true essence.

Judgments

As we proceed through Stage Four, we need to be especially careful about harboring judgments regarding the "right" and "wrong" or "good" and "bad" of our actions and attitudes. Otherwise, once again we will find ourselves engaging in Stage Two reasoning.

We may well make a statement like "I no longer accept this situation and want to make changes." This statement is very different from saying, "I have been wrong by doing this; it was no good." Making judgments is not appropriate in Stage Four. When we move through Stage Four, we realize that in reality there is no judgment.

What was previously thought of as wrong is simply no longer acceptable to us.

For example, Tina is now in the fourth stage of healing regarding her relationship with her husband, Tom. He has a drinking problem and is rarely at home. One evening he came home late and Tina said to him, "Tom, I know you have been having difficulty at work, but I have been having trouble with your staying out late and drinking with your friends. I love you very dearly and I have been suffering and crying a lot. But I have reached a point where I simply can't do this to myself or our relationship anymore. I cannot remain in the role of the 'good wife,' staying home while my husband is detached from me, abuses himself, and abuses our relationship. I would like to work things out with you, but I will no longer tolerate the way things have become." Tina's statement reflects the nature of the magnitude of healing inherent in Stage Four. It involves a realization, which carries a powerful weight.

For Tom, Stage Four presents an important bifurcation point as well. He must either decide to continue with his old patterns or realize that he must make changes in his life if he wants to keep his marriage from falling apart. If both partners in the relationship are in Stage Four, they can proceed on their healing journey as a couple. However, if they are at different stages, the situation becomes more challenging and complex. The relationship may become more chaotic and the friction more intense.

This could lead to accelerated healing of one partner and, therefore, the relationship, or the relationship may have to end because one partner moves ahead with the healing process while the other remains mired in the same stage of healing. This situation does not make one partner a saint and the other a villain. Instead, it produces a just consequence: the appropriate stage of healing for both of them.

Skipping Steps

As some people reach the "I'm mad as hell . . ." part of Stage

Four, in their zeal to react against their dishonored selves they may choose to discharge their distressing patterns and attachments without taking the necessary intervening steps. They may move from early Stage Four directly into Stage Seven, attempting resolution through a state of discharge. However, this does not produce the wholeness, healing, or resolution that occurs if Stages Five and Six are experienced first.

A Commitment to Wholeness

Immediately after we have decided "I am not going to take this anymore," it is important to confirm our commitment to wholeness rather than act on that commitment. Family and friends will often say to us, "Now that you've decided you don't want to take it anymore, think things over a bit." What I suggest is that a person not think it over or take any action. When we say, "I don't want to take it anymore," we are ready to just *feel* our desire to regain our personal power — nothing more.

Moving Through Stage Four

At the beginning of Stage Four, we commonly feel anxious, upset, irritable, or angry without knowing why. We are aware that we are stuck in a perspective, but we have not yet removed enough interference from our bodymind to reclaim our power. We are still feeling powerlessness in response to reclaiming our true identity and selfhood, because our system has not yet made the commitment that "I won't take this anymore. I deserve more than this."

When we have become disconnected from, or have denied the reality of, our internal power — or if we have not expressed our innate potential — we often become angry, best expressed by the line "I'm mad as hell!" However, as we move through Stage Four, the initial irritation, upset, or anger is gradually replaced by a deep sense of self-respect and the desire to truly honor who we are. Anger is replaced by an acceptance of the idea that "I just have to do this now," without the angry charge we experienced earlier.

Sarah, whose case we already discussed, experienced this aspect of Stage Four. While lying in her hospital bed after her second angioplasty, Sarah began to see that her old perspectives regarding self-image, diet, and exercise had brought her face-to-face with a life-threatening heart condition. She had gone through a period of anger. Her statement "How could I have done this to myself?" was later replaced with "I can't go on like this any longer." With the latter statement, she set the stage for important changes in her life.

We know we are moving through Stage Four effectively when there is no longer an angry charge to reclaiming our power and we don't feel we have to act on reclaiming it. When Stage Four is completed, we will have integrated its lessons fully into our consciousness. As a result, we will automatically begin to move directly away from the suffering. If Stage Four is not fully completed, we will walk away from the suffering and not confront what was behind the illusion that caused the suffering in the first place.

At the end of Stage Four, we become aware that we need to go back to our darkness and reexperience the time of the original suffering. We must go back and contact whatever we have decided we will not take anymore. For when we say, "Hey, I don't want this anymore," we need to actually see what it is that we don't want. By the time we reach this phase, we feel strong enough and separate enough from the suffering so that we can visit the "old neighborhood" again without moving back. We have the inner strength to return and look at the photo album of experiences without being a part of them anymore. As a result, we give ourselves the opportunity to gain more insight from them as we prepare to move toward the fifth stage of healing, which involves merging.

For The Practitioner

As in Stage Three, this point in the healing process will often draw people into offices of subluxation-based or "straight" chiropractors, holistic physicians, bodyworkers, and psychotherapists of many different types. People moving into Stage Four often come to my office to have their spines checked for interference. With only a little care, they may reexperience traumatic events at deep levels, reclaim their power, and make major life-changing decisions. They are ripe for change.

Many people may choose the elective surgery they had been considering to help resolve whatever underlying distortion they may have. Some may decide to undergo minor plastic surgery, like a rhinoplasty or a tummy tuck, or a more serious type of operation. John C. Pierrakos, M.D., observed this process after his wife, Eva, the founder of a spiritual community known as The Pathwork, had a mastectomy:

> What I remember is Eva telling me later that the [operation] propelled her into a new place, and this had a lot to do with forming a new group. She told me that the operation had an enormous effect on her, almost like a reincarnation, a rebirth. She said something like, "I felt completely changed after that."

My co-author, Nathaniel, went through a similar, yet less intense experience. He had suffered an inguinal hernia during a period of emotional stress over whether or not to sell the family home after his mother's death. During eighteen months his discomfort increased while his ability to walk or stand became more limited. He became concerned about weight gain and possible ill health from a lack of exercise. After an important spiritual awakening in Brazil, he decided to put the house up for sale and have the hernia surgically repaired. The operation represented an end of a period of suffering and the beginning of a phase of greater self-awareness and inner growth.

Whatever the outer action or procedure may be, in Stage Four we have now given ourself permission to move on and have a stronger, more unified sense of self.

From Patient to Practice Member

In the early stages of the healing process (Stages One, Two, and Three), we may seek the services of a doctor or therapist to end our suffering, manage our discomfort, or bring order to our life again. In these stages, the main task of the physician, psychotherapist or other practitioner involves helping us recreate life the way it was just before our symptoms arose and the illness or the suffering inter-rupted our orderly existence.

In Stage Four, we walk through an important door. Here, our personal power and integrity — the "I am" consciousness within us, our inner wisdom, and the essential rhythms we express — must be honored. We no longer want to return to the way life was before the suffering, because we are now aware that much of the old life was-n't working for us.

As a consequence of this new awareness, we are more inclined to seek practitioners who will help us experience more wholeness in our lives, and enable us to honor our essence more completely. There may still be a need for a practitioner who can make us "feel better," but this help is now administered within the context of an evolving self. We now want a relationship where the physician or therapist helps us take back our power rather than an authority fig-ure who is in control of the situation while we remain passive. In the fourth stage of healing, we are now ready for a more co-creative relationship with the healing facilitator.

Since I began working with people who were moving through Stage Four, I have felt uncomfortable with the term patient. Accord-ing to *Taber's Cyclopedic Medical Dictionary,* a patient is "one who is sick with, or being treated for, an illness or injury" or "an individ-ual receiving medical care." The term implies that people are sick and that I, as the practitioner, will provide treatment to make them well. But I believe we are our own healers, so I decided to use a dif-ferent term for those involved in the higher stages of the healing process.

In my Network Chiropractic office, I called people who were

taking their power back "practice members." They were members of my practice who see that their growth, healing, and evolution are primary. The distinction is this: patients want to be "fixed" and returned to the way they were before the onset of symptoms; practice members no longer find this place acceptable.

The twelve stages of healing are not just intellectual concepts that one can theorize about, understand, and move through. This simply cannot be done from the rational mind alone. True movement occurs when spiritual growth results from living through the experience. It is the difference between watching a baseball game and being at bat yourself. It is the difference between saying "hot" to a child who is about to touch a stove and the child being burned and discovering what "hot" is. It is the difference between describing what a taste of chocolate is like and tasting the chocolate yourself. Like life, each stage of the healing journey is experiential. It is practical and it is real, although not always convenient.

One intent of this book is to help empower patients, practice members, and healing facilitators to better understand and communicate their needs. Because much healing occurs beyond the third stage, it is important that healing facilitators understand there are practice members out there who need their assistance. Communication and methods used must be radically different from the way practitioners ordinarily approach patients. Unlike patients, practice members do not want to be limited in their approach to healing. In Stage Four, practice members want to be set free; they want to take their power back.

Toward Stage Five

In Stage Four, there is an awareness of what we desire, and then life provides us with the means of achieving it. At first we say, "No, I won't take this anymore," the "taking this" referring to giving away our power. With that affirmative — "I won't" — the sense of self-hood (the "I am" presence) is strengthened. Our sense of self is now strong enough to move us into Stage Five, which involves our ability to face up to the illusion or experience of distress, even if it does not yet seem like an illusion.

Hearing Yourself Ask for Help

In the earlier part of Stage Four, you may use words like, "Please, don't make me take this anymore. Please don't make me have to put up with this any longer." Although this may sound like the dialogue in Stage One, your sense of self is strong enough that you ask for help for yourself. In Stage One, there is only the experience of suffering. There is no awareness of an individual doing the suffering. In Stage Four, it is different.

Later in Stage Four, you may say "Please don't let me dishonor myself anymore" or "Please guide me in honoring myself."

Stage Four Exercise

Place your finger over your left nostril. Breathe quickly in through your right nostril, then quickly exhale through your right nostril. Now place your finger over your right nostril. Breathe quickly in through your left nostril, then quickly breathe out through your left nostril. Continue alternate nostril breathing for at least two minutes.

Meanwhile, place your free hand on your chest. Feel your chest rise and fall as you breathe. Slowly move your hand down to areas that do not feel as though they are moving with your breathing. Then move back to those areas that are moving.

Stage Four Declarations

"I take my power back."
"I honor my total being."
"I reclaim my wholeness."

Stage Four Exercise

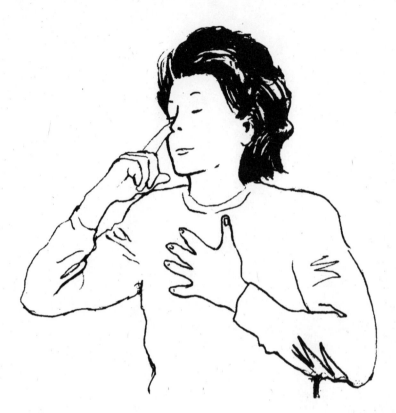

5

STAGE FIVE

Merging with the Illusion

"I wish to go back to my place and see my beast again."
— BEAUTY IN "BEAUTY AND THE BEAST"

The fifth stage of healing involves merging with the fears, pains, illusions, and concerns behind the suffering. It is a rite of passage that calls upon us to confront these aspects of our self from a place of strength and from the sincere desire for wholeness we developed in Stage Four. Separation from either your light or dark side of yourself will produce suffering. With merging, the part of our nature we have alienated, disliked, or ignored is integrated into the rest of our being.

For many people, Stage Five will be a time to merge with their dark side or their shadow. Others have spent a considerable amount of time with their shadow and are all too familiar with it. For this group of people, Stage Five will be a time to move past the illusion which kept them from their light or their goodness. After you have gone through Stage Five several times in your life, it becomes more common to merge with your separated goodness or light.

Merging is generally not supported or practiced in Western culture. Yet facing up to and eventually merging with one's shadow self are important aspects of initiation rites, puberty rites, healing rituals, and other sacred ceremonies among native peoples throughout the world. In North America, the Sun Dance is perhaps the most well known. Traditionally practiced by Plains Indians, including the Arapahoe, Cherokee, and Dakota, it has sometimes been called the "Gazing-at-the-Sun-Dance." This ceremony is undertaken by only the bravest and most worthy of tribal members in order to fulfill a vow to the sun, regarded as the source of all life and wisdom.

The Sun Dance is often misunderstood by Westerners, who focus on the self-torture, flesh piercing, and bondage that are often part of this ritual. However, the essential role of these practices is to promote humility, purification, surrender, and merging beyond one's limiting illusions. By "giving one's body to the source of life," the dancers hope to receive visions of enlightenment and healing through contact with their spirit guardians.

The vision quest is also an important Native American tradition. It involves long periods of fasting, prayer, and sacrifice. In this rite of passage, a person goes to an isolated place and spends up to five days fasting and praying in order to receive a vision from the spirit world that will bring greater wholeness and direction to their life. As many of us remember from our childhood years, being alone in nature, totally cut off from family and friends, can bring up some of our deepest fears, like abandonment, danger, and death. By bravely facing one's fears and merging with them, the person on the vision quest moves the veil of illusion aside and merges with what lies beyond.

In the Western esoteric spiritual tradition, confronting the "Dweller on the Threshold" is parallel to these native traditions. According to *Esoteric Psychology* by Alice Bailey,

> The Dweller is the "one who stands before the gate of God," who dwells in the shadow of the portal of initiation. . . . The Dweller can be defined as the sum total of the forces of the lower nature of the personality, prior to illumination, to inspiration and to initiation.

The story lines of many fairy tales reflect the importance of courageously facing and merging with one's shadow self, or animal nature, to achieve power, wholeness, and selfhood. Jack slaying the giant in "Jack and the Beanstalk," Hansel and Gretel killing the cruel witch, and the marriage of Beauty to the Beast symbolically illustrate the importance of overcoming fear of the hidden side of our nature and merging with it in order to live "happily ever after."

Ernest Kurtz and Katherine Ketcham addressed this issue in their book, *The Spirituality of Imperfection:*

> Because paradox is at our very core, the spirituality of imperfection suggests that only by embracing the "dark side" of our ambiguous natures can we ever come to know "the light." We find ourselves only by giving up our selves, we gain freedom by submitting to the will of others, we gain autonomy not by insisting on our own rights. Saints and sages throughout the centuries have maintained that it is in this willingness to give up the self and give in to others that the road to human wholeness can be found. And for those who would give up "self," the first step is to give up certainty.

Whenever we journey through the healing process, there comes a time when we have the opportunity to face, learn from, and merge with these alienated aspects of our being so that we can move toward wholeness. By doing so, we continually face aspects of the dweller, which stands at the gate of a greater reality. Stage Five offers us this opportunity. And this process is essential for the stages of healing that are to follow.

Entering Stage Five

Stage Five involves revisiting the place where our suffering began. In Stage Five, we not only observe the process behind the suffering, we also experience the process with a stronger sense of self. We know that we are separate from our distress or the source of our suffering as opposed to being the suffering, as we were in Stage One. As a result, we can merge with the illusion of suffering without "taking it personally."

Merging with one's suffering, excuses, or illusions, as opposed to competing with them, is the antithesis of the therapeutic model practiced by most physicians, psychologists and other symptom-oriented practitioners, who are primarily geared toward moving away from the chaos and toward restoring "order" through drugs, surgery, behavior modification, body manipulation, and psychoanalysis.

Perhaps the only socially acceptable ways of merging in our culture is through the process of natural childbirth or when we work out strenuously at the health club. During natural childbirth, the mother breathes deeply, moves with the rhythm of the contractions, and eventually merges beyond her pain as she brings forth a new life. While repeating the mantra "No pain, no gain," people often merge by forcing the bodymind to move beyond their physical and psychological limits. They are not merging with the source of their suffering per se, but they are recognizing that they have to push themselves past the illusions of their limits.

However, those of us who reach the fifth stage of healing need to work with the experience of suffering, pain, or chaos rather than compete with it. To heal, we must look at what is behind the chaos and invest our energy in getting to know it better. By the time we reach Stage Five, we are able to comfortably merge with our source of discomfort and discover what it has to teach us.

As a natural consequence of Network Chiropractic care, my colleagues and I have found that people will often spontaneously merge with the source of their suffering while three inner events take place:

1. The mechanical tension on the spinal cord releases when it becomes free of interference.
2. The nervous system remembers the position that the spine

was in when the original trauma occurred.

3. The nervous system reexperiences the event with new insight.

When this process is guided by our internal wisdom and not by our educated minds, the results can be profound. We revisit the experience of a traumatic event from an expanded perspective and an inner desire to be one with the trauma. We saw this process take place with Arthur, the boat captain who reexperienced a traumatic attack by his father. He went through suffering and saw both the trauma he suffered and the pattern it produced in his bodymind. This permitted him to merge with the experience on physical, emotional, mental, and even spiritual levels.

Being Reborn

Frank was a conservative professional in his mid-forties. He describes the following experience he had in a healing facilitator's office:

> I was in the room for at least 45 minutes, experiencing a great deal of discomfort in my upper neck. My body began jumping up and down, moving from side to side. I was in utter anguish and was stuck in it. This went on for perhaps 30 minutes, although I lost track of time. At one point my arms bent back at the elbow (I was on my back) and my fingers took on a claw-like position. I was breathing rapidly in and out of my mouth, feeling as though I was in some kind of hell. My arms began flailing around violently. I suddenly realized I was in the birth canal, struggling to move forward and get out. This lasted for some time until what seemed like a climax occurred, followed by relief. I knew I had just relived my birth. There was no question in my mind.

After this event, Frank felt a great sense of relief, and his life took on greater purpose. He then experienced the event several more times, with less intensity. Somehow, when visiting the place past the anguish, which was reflected as suffering in many areas of his life, Frank came to a greater state of self-knowing. One important aspect of his story is that Frank experienced body movements, awareness-es, and breathing that had a rhythm beyond his control. After he merged with the experience, he knew what it was about. He could not figure it out consciously. There was no logic. It just unfolded to his conscious mind as he literally clawed past the illusion.

Darlene's Story

Darlene came to my office for her first adjustment. After exam-ining her spine, I asked if a traumatic event had occurred in her life sixteen years earlier. She couldn't recall an event, but I made a note of my findings in her clinical record.

After three or four spinal adjustments, she began to reexperience her stepfather raping her sixteen years earlier. As her spinal system was becoming free of interference, it "remembered" the traumatic event and Darlene actually merged with it. As a consequence of that merging, she experienced tremendous anger toward her stepfather, which lasted for a couple of days. She chose to consult a personal-abuse counselor, and because Darlene was able to merge with her suffering, she soon totally forgave her stepfather.

Darlene later related that the same evening she had forgiven him, he phoned to say he was sorry. That was the first time they had spo-ken since shortly after the rape. As a result of Darlene's nervous sys-tem merging with the source of her suffering, she changed her per-spective and viewed her experience from a "higher" state of consciousness. This new perspective created a change in her life that her stepfather somehow responded to. This kind of experience, in which an emotional attachment to an event is released after merg-ing with it, somehow produces an effect on others involved in the drama.

Roger's Story

Roger called me the morning after I had given him three spinal adjustments, asking if I could see him again right away. He was "going through some real tough stuff." A short while later I walked into Roger's room and found him in a cold sweat, his body shaking and his hands trembling. He was crying, which he never did. This was a cry deep from the soul. With a wastebasket in front of him, Roger was on all fours, retching violently and grunting deeply from his core. This wailing grunt was the kind of sound that comes from being punched in the lower gut. He was rocking back and forth and was sobbing between dry heaves.

One could say that Roger was very ill and needed immediate medical attention, but Roger was actually in the fifth stage of healing. Knowing that his nervous system was free of interference, I realized that his apparent illness was an expression of his innate intelligence setting him free from previously unresolved life events that had been lodged in his nervous system and bodymind.

Roger had repressed his emotions through much of his life. He had once sought relief through drugs, and about a dozen years earlier, he had gone through heroin addiction withdrawal. Now he was reexperiencing the withdrawal and detoxification he thought he had completed.

Later that day, Roger said that when he had released the deep low cries that alternated with his sobbing, an underlying tension that had always been present disappeared. Roger now saw his world through new eyes as he gave himself over to a process that appeared to have a rhythm of its own. As a result of surrendering to this process, he experienced a state of peace he had never known before.

Not everyone can move through Stage Five like Frank, Darlene, and Roger. In Ron's situation — which we described in Stage Three — merging was not an option open to him. Ron's bodymind had not been healed enough to merge with the trauma. Perhaps if the healing process had begun earlier, his nervous system would have grown stronger and more flexible to accommodate the stage of merging. But at his stage of the healing process, merging with the source of his suffering was more frightening to him than anything else.

Beyond The Veil of Illusion

When we merge with our suffering, we realize that we have been living in an illusion. The person we see now is not the person we thought we knew. The person we interacted with before merging does not react the way we expected. The experience we revisit is not the same as we remembered. When we merge with our illusion, we feel a new sense of empowerment on intellectual, spiritual, and emotional levels. This strength comes from discovering the truth about certain aspects of our being that lie beyond the veil of illusion.

As with all discovery, the time must be right. Asking ourselves to merge with our suffering before we have completed the earlier stages of healing is neither physically nor emotionally sound. A psychotherapist, for example, may have a patient merge with suffering through hypnosis and introduce suggestions designed to bring the person back to a traumatic experience with only a "safe" amount of material being remembered. However, merging cannot be forced and can only occur safely when the bodymind is ready to merge.

There is a difference between intentionally moving back into one's alienated self in order to merge and spontaneously merging as a natural occurrence. Merging comes about naturally as interference in the spinal system and the connective tissues is removed. Merging is not intentional. We do not know it is occurring until after we are immersed in it.

Merging is a surreal dream in which time and space are warped. We can sit by a lake and experience an event that may have occurred in another part of the world forty years earlier. As we surrender to the sense of suspended time and space, we become aware that it is a major spiritual portal for healing *right now*. To quote from Ernest Kurtz and Katherine Ketcham,

In weakness strength is discovered; in wretchedness, joy; in the "abyss of nothingness," the "fruit of grace." And so we need not escape ourselves to find peace or joy, for while spirituality is always *beyond*, it is discovered first within.

The importance of merging is expressed in the fairy tale "Beauty and the Beast." Beauty has consistently rejected the Beast's pleas for marriage because she is repelled by his coarse, ugly appearance. But during a dream a handsome prince appeared and said "with a voice that went straight to her heart,"

> Ah, Beauty! you are not so unfortunate as you suppose. Here you will be rewarded for all you have suffered elsewhere. Your every wish shall be gratified. Only try to find me out, no matter how I might be disguised, as I love you dearly, and in making me happy, you will find your own happiness. Be as true-hearted as you are beautiful, and we shall have nothing left to wish for. . . . Only do not let yourself be deceived by appearances.

Eventually, Beauty agreed to marry (merge with) the Beast. As soon as she declared her intentions, the Beast suddenly disappeared and the handsome prince stood in its place. Through merging from a place of love, she lifted the curse that was placed upon the Beast, and they "lived happily ever after." This story teaches that by merging with the "beast within," we become whole again, and we initiate a cycle of healing and growth in our lives.

A women named Charlotte, for example, is in Stage Five and has chosen to confront a difficult aspect of her relationship. She initiates a conversation with her partner and says, "You know, I haven't felt loved when I have been with you lately. It is very hurtful and I'd like to change it."

Charlotte may begin to feel the pain in her relationship, and at that point she merges with it and experiences loneliness (whether she is with her partner or not). As she experiences the loneliness, Charlotte somehow starts to observe it as though she is now separate from it.

This was something Charlotte could not do in Stage One. Then, she could not observe the loneliness without being attached to it. As she merged with the experience from a place of greater selfhood, she was able to observe it, experience it, and feel as though she was swimming in the ocean of loneliness. Yet, as the swimmer, she was separate from it.

Deeply feeling any experience may activate feelings and memories of other experiences. Eventually, we find that we are moving behind the veil of illusion we thought was real. It is an experience we were not in touch with, and as a result we didn't know what it had to teach us. It may have been a concept we were not conscious of, an experience we did not understand, or a trauma we had not yet dealt with. In Stage Five we realize that this experience lies behind the suffering, behind the dishonoring, and behind the false sense of self. As we merge with it, we more fully discover how we have disconnected from ourselves, and we become more aware of our power and the fact that we are responsible for what is happening in our lives.

Donald's Story

I have been adjusting people's spines for nearly twenty years. I enjoy being a chiropractor, and people respond in a positive way to my work. Yet not too long ago, I began to experience a severe pain in my left arm whenever I was adjusting people, even while giving gentle adjustments. With a room full of people waiting, I would often go into the bathroom to cry because the pain in my arm was so great.

Because I had already gone through the suffering and had moved through stages Two, Three, and Four, I was able to look at the pain in a different way. In Stage Five, one reason why we are finally able to merge is that we no longer see ourselves as victims.

We no longer take our suffering personally; we view suffering as a wake-up call to look at ourselves and our situations more deeply.

Rather than seeing my pain as an enemy, now an awareness within me said, "Wake up and give your attention to this. You cannot continue going in the direction you are without undesirable consequences. You may have exceeded your safety limits. Something has to change."

I looked at my arm while I said to myself "This really hurts," but at the same time I was both interested and curious. Rather than judge the symptoms as being wrong, I asked, "What is my body trying to say to me?" And as I asked I looked at the arm, and rather than see that my arm was killing me, I realized that it was I who was killing my arm. Some aspect of my bodymind — or some aspect of my past — was not working for me. As I held my arm, I suddenly realized that the pain was not because I was sick, but because I was needy. In the context of therapy someone looks for answers or excuses; in the spiritual context of healing, someone looks for understanding and often forgiveness.

I then asked, "What is it?" "What do you want?" and for a fleeting moment experienced a feeling of sadness. I then began to cry as though I were a child and someone had taken my favorite toy. And when I looked at my arm, I felt the pain switching off intermittently with my episodes of crying.

Like Little Red Riding Hood, who looked at grandma with the hunch that "this may not be as it seems," I sensed that my pain was more than I had perceived it to be. I then visualized myself as Donald walking into my arm or swimming within my arm, having a hunch that I needed to look deeper, carefully observing what I was seeing and feeling. Images of my childhood began to appear between the flashes of pain, and I began to feel an overwhelming sense of sorrow. When I experienced the sorrow, the physical pain disappeared. I did not judge these feelings or say to myself "So this is the reason why I have pain," nor did I make a statement like "I am hurting because I felt inadequate as a child." At this point I merged with what was behind the suffering and became aware of feelings of sorrow and inadequacy from my childhood I had not seen before.

Merging typifies my concept of healing, which is wholeness — perceiving all the parts and respecting them, regardless of their past, and inviting them to participate with us. With merging we feel more and can therefore heal whatever is behind our experience of suffering. At this point we need not know what to do about our discovery or even understand the significance of it. When we merge with the illusion, we know inwardly what is behind it. We may not be consciously aware of what we know, nor do we have to. We simply observe ourselves during our interaction with our suffering. Again, it is like going back to the neighborhoods we lived in as children and spending some time there, yet knowing we don't need to live there anymore.

Encountering the Stillness

A woman in Stage Five may experience menstrual cramps, for example. While feeling the intensity of the cramps, she is suffering and asks "Why me?" But, in the middle of her pain the cramps grab her attention and say "Look here." So she looks. Because she has progressed to Stage Five, her sense of self is strong enough and her nervous system is flexible enough for her to actually move "in between" the cramps. From this vantage point, she observes and feels. Nothing more needs to be done. All that is needed is to withhold judgment, be open to observing the drama, and feel what she is feeling at the moment.

Merging with the images, fears, and illusions allows us to encounter the stillness that lies within, beyond the fears and pain. As we move in between the feelings of the menstrual cramps, the inadequacy, the shame, the fear, the drug addiction, the pain, or the breathing difficulty associated with asthma, we move to a point of observing it. It is as though we place our whole self within the inadequacy, the addictive behavior, or the lungs, and from that area we look around.

Welcome to the Family

Behind the suffering we often find a hurt "child consciousness" that has not grown up with the rest of our being. Like an angry child, this immature consciousness has its demands and needs irrespective of whether they work for the benefit of the whole organism or "family." By crying "My needs must be met," this aspect of ourselves is living out an agenda that has not yet grown up. Perhaps it is the part of us that says, "I want attention now" or "I have to produce this stomach acid."

Whatever the reality is, our bodies are acting from a small sense, a small circle of self based upon a limited, immature perspective. As we observe ourselves and merge with what is beyond the distress, we invite that aspect of our being to grow up. We invite that child to become part of the family again. We ask that alienated aspect of ourselves to merge with and work for the greater good of the whole. Stage Five offers the opportunity for that fragmented aspect of ourselves we have not served well to be viewed by the whole being. As we observe that consciousness, it observes itself and helps to set us free.

At the beginning of the merging process, we may experience graphic and highly charged situations that may involve violence and cruelty. But, because we now have a greater sense of self, we can dispassionately observe these dramas without becoming identified with, or attached to, them.

Later in the merging process, we will begin to distinguish between the points of agitation and the points of stillness. And as we merge through this stage several times — which naturally occurs at different moments in the healing journey — we will easily be guided into the space of stillness that lies between the areas of suffering. Rather than moving into the core of agitation or illusion, we now merge into the core of our stillness. This place of peace within the suffering is an area of rest between the periods of outer chaos. It is a rest stop during the healing journey.

Arlene's Story

Arlene's experience offers a profound illustration of the transformation of merging. Arlene had been experiencing severe abdominal cramps for more than a year. Her suffering brought up strong fears that she had cancer and that she was going to die. She had undergone several extensive medical examinations involving dozens of tests, yet nothing wrong could be found. Although part of her was relieved at these findings, another part was distressed because the doctors couldn't find the reason behind her pain and suffering. Arlene's preoccupation with the cramps took up so much of her attention that both her career and her social life were affected.

After a while, Arlene became aware that there were patterns involved in the onset of the cramps, and she realized that she was stuck in a perspective, although she did not yet know what the perspective was. She also felt that she had to make changes in her life, but she did not yet know what they were. One day Arlene said to herself, "There's no way I can accept this situation anymore. I won't accept the cramps and I won't accept whatever is behind the cramps. I deserve more than this." Her words reflect a typical Stage Four response.

At the advice of a healing facilitator, she decided to observe the cramps and "look inside" her abdomen not as a victim, but as an interested, curious observer. She looked at the cramps and saw nothing at first, but knew there was something lurking. She soon began to see some color taking form. She then asked the area, "What do you want?" and received no answer.

Because the vision was an aspect of Arlene's consciousness and therefore a part of her, it must eventually answer her question. It will answer her from the perspective it has. If, for example, we ask a three-year-old a question, the child will answer from its perspective. If we ask a ten-year-old and a fifty-year-old the same question, they will answer from their perspectives. So, when we ask an aspect of our consciousness a question, it will respond according to its ability to know.

Arlene then said, "You are waking me up, you are letting me know pain. What do you want?" She repeated the question several times until she heard an answer. And the answer was, "I want to kill you. I want to give you cancer. I want to destroy you."

At first, the response was terrifying and Arlene began to cry. But she said, "I want to see what you look like," because she sincerely wanted to reach out and understand the alienated aspect of her consciousness that wanted her to die. To her surprise, she saw a little rabbit. She laughed, feeling relieved that there was nothing to worry about.

Her healing facilitator suggested that she look into the eyes of the rabbit. As she looked, she saw that it was a monster stabbing her abdomen. Knowing that it wanted to kill her, she asked the demon, "What will you get out of killing me?" and to her surprise it replied, "I will be acknowledged and accepted."

She then said, "So it is peace you are looking for?" and the demon replied, "Yes." Arlene began to cry. She reached out to this alienated aspect of her being and invited it to merge with the rest of her so they could all have peace. At the same time, she promised that she would never ignore its needs again. With this declaration the cramps flared up again and then subsided but it was not the end of her pain. Although her "condition" improved significantly, this merging was not a magical answer. In her healing, she visited stages One through Five several times, often with greater understanding.

Shortly after this profound experience, Arlene realized that she had become more powerful than ever before. She knew she had to make changes in her life on a deep level, but did not know what those changes needed to be. By the time she reached Stage Five, a great deal of healing had already taken place, and as a result, there had been spiritual growth. The connection with her spiritual side enabled her to merge with her inner demon, an aspect of the dweller, that part of her consciousness from which she had been alienated. The inner "knowing that she knew" then brought her to the sixth stage of healing.

Often, the moment of encountering our shadow self is what religious teachers call the dark night of the soul. To move ahead in the healing journey, these demons must be faced. By the time we reach the fifth stage of healing, we have both the strength and the courage to surrender to what we were afraid to face. And soon after the moment of surrender, we begin to encounter the Light. This experience is beautifully expressed by Bernadette Roberts in *The Path to the No-Self*:

> With no place else to go, nowhere else to turn, we have no choice but to go down to the depths of our nothingness, where, at rock bottom, God eventually reveals Himself and discloses to us the rootedness of our existence to Him. Thus having travelled through the bottomless void of our being, we eventually come to rest in a deep union with God — the abiding stillpoint at the center of our being.

Therapeutic Intervention

I have mentioned that the conventional practice of medicine does not leave room for the individual to merge with distress and move beyond its appearance except during natural childbirth. Sometimes pain-killing drugs cannot be used for certain painful medical or dental procedures. The individual is told to bite down on an object or use meditation to feel the pain or to merge with it. However, this practice is rare.

The medical profession views the experience of suffering as chaos that disrupts a life of order and balance. The traditional physician or psychotherapist wants to bring order back and eliminate the chaos; for why would an individual want to merge with chaos if chaos is seen as evil while order is seen as godly? It would be as though merging into chaos is like merging with evil itself. However, until we are able to merge with whatever is behind our illusions, there can be no resolution. The illusions merely gain strength when we fail to face them or try to resist them.

The idea of merging is an integral part of many forms of body-work, including bioenergetics, Core Energetics, Trager, Zero Balancing, Ida Rolf's Structural Integration (Rolfing), shiatsu, deep-tissue massage, Network Chiropractic, and several schools of yoga. Merging is also an aspect of Pre-Cognitive Re-Education, Rebirthing, Holodynamics, psychodrama, Primal Therapy, and various forms of transpersonal psychology. Certain spiritual and religious disciplines view merging as an essential aspect of achieving union with God, bringing us past the shadow of illusion to the light behind the form.

Merging commonly occurs in a dream state, as it did when the Beast visited Beauty in her sleep and told her to look beyond her illusions. In Jungian analysis and other forms of psychological therapy, merging while in the dream state is a major portal to healing. Those following a spiritual discipline will also often keep dream journals because they appreciate the importance of merging with the fuller range of consciousness available in the dream state. Movies, myths, opera, and dance may also provide opportunities for us to merge vicariously with characters who activate our self-awareness.

Fear of Fear

Much of our resistance to merging with suffering pertains to fear. Mary was always afraid of elevators and refused to ride in them. She experienced fear every time she thought about them. One day, while Mary and her brother were in a department store, he dragged her into an elevator. As she was forced into it, she screamed, "No, no, no, I'm afraid!" although after the elevator began moving, she realized she was no longer frightened. Her fear involved approaching the experience of riding the elevator rather than the experience itself.

The aspects we are not ready to merge with often sabotage our relationships, rob us of our power and trust, and impair our health. Yet, when we surrender ourselves completely to the rhythm of what we are going through, there can be no fear. Fear is usually connected to the illusion of what we imagine will happen rather than to the reality of a situation.

Many of us are afraid of going bankrupt, or that our partner will leave us, or that we will have a life-threatening disease and die. Our fear is enhanced by trying to avoid the situation that is associated with our illusions, our distress, and our suffering. When we begin to merge, however, we ask ourselves, "What is the worst thing that can happen?" The worst that can happen is that we can go broke, lose our partner, or get sick and die.

This does not minimize the significance of such uncomfortable possibilities, and they are aspects of life many of us go through. But when we disempower the illusion by merging with it, we suddenly change our relationship with it. New perspectives and new realities can then come from the other side of our illusion.

Finding out what lies behind the pattern of illusion, knowing what has to be done differently, and how our lives are to change can only be seen when we observe the situation clearly and without illusions. And we come upon these realizations through the stage of merging.

Hearing Yourself Ask for Help

In Stage Five, asking for help or praying reflects preoccupation with mastering your illusion or confronting your darkness. Therefore, we may say something like, "God, help me confront my shadow. Help me make peace with my darkness. Please help me move past my illusions. Help me find the truth behind this."

Stage Five Exercise

Frank's Rebirthing experience mentioned earlier includes breathing and body movements consistent with merging. In this exercise your hands may take claw-like positions or may move in spirals or swirls. As you rock your arms and legs in a synchronous fashion, the rhythm that overtakes you will guide your movements. At times your arms or legs may stop moving. Often, this is the center of the illusion.

Lie comfortably on your back and bring your arms over your chest area. Slowly swirl both hands in circular motions between your chest and over your head. Breathe deeply in and out through your mouth, striving to synchronize your breathing with the hand motions over your chest. There should be no restrictions to your hands moving over your head and no tension in your arms or shoulders.

Bend your knees. Let your hips and legs sway gently from side to side. Gradually synchronize the movement of your upper and lower limbs with your breathing.

Then, let your arms assume any movement they need to make, and permit this movement to connect to whatever movement your legs need to do. Let the rhythm take over.

Now look into the part of yourself that you have identified with the process of suffering. Say hello to the region, and gently touch it. Then say, "What do you want?" Wait for a response. Then reply, "You may have all the acknowledgment you ever wanted."

Stage Five Declarations

"I welcome all of my parts and experiences."

"I join with my inner family."

"I merge with my shadow self."

"I merge with my goodness and light."

"I embrace every aspect of my being."

Stage Five Exercise

6

STAGE SIX

Preparation for Resolution

I am flexible. I am building momentum.
I am ready. It is OK to let go.

Stage Six is both an action and transitional stage. It helps the bodymind become more flexible so we can discharge and resolve trapped perspectives, memories, information, energy, and patterns. These aspects of our being are no longer able to adapt to our new and stronger sense of self and therefore must be released. The release will occur at the discretion of our innate wisdom, when our nervous system becomes free of interference and our bodymind becomes flexible enough to accommodate major change.

By the time we move from Stage Five, we have gained an awareness of what is behind our illusions, even if this awareness is not conscious. At the same time, our sense of self has been strengthened because we have gone into the belly of the whale or have been eaten by the big, bad wolf and merged with our fear to move beyond it. In fact, the previous stage of healing is not unlike the story of Moses leading the Jews through the Red Sea. The water didn't part until it was at their nostrils (talk about merging!). Like the Jews who risked the prospect of drowning, facing our greatest fears in Stage Five made us stronger and more empowered to take the next step in our healing journey.

Stage Six involves the awareness that the dissonant aspects of our lives — the sources of our suffering — are about to be relinquished. It is the kind of feeling we may have when we become nauseated before we throw up, when we are about to have a bowel movement or when a powerful sneeze is coming on. For some, it can manifest as the uneasy feeling we have before telling our partners that our relationship is over. Of course, the feelings produced in Stage Six are not always unpleasant. The gradual buildup of tension and excitement before orgasm has much in common with the feelings this stage can bring up, as preparation for resolution moves into high gear.

Stage Six provides us with the flexibility and increasing momentum we need to allow the changes we want in our life to occur. It is one of the more dynamic stages in the healing process, and can often be moved through quickly. Larry Dossey, M.D., describes this movement as an essential component of health in his book *Space, Time and Medicine:*

> Health is harmony, and harmony has no meaning without the fluid movement of interdependent parts. Like a stream that becomes stagnant when it ceases to flow, harmony and health turn into disease and death when stasis occurs. We return to the concept of the biodance, the endless streaming of the body-in-flux.

More Than a Preparatory Stage

Stage Six involves more than preparation for the discharge and resolution which takes place in Stage Seven. The essential rhythm of Stage Six involves centering and grounding our bodymind's energy so it is prepared if discharge becomes necessary. This centering brings the awareness that discharge is a welcome and appropriate event in our healing journey. Knowing there is a buildup of tension that must be released — while experiencing dissonant or alienated rhythm within that must eventually resolve itself — is a very important aspect of healing.

In many cases, we may be able to resolve our dissonant or alienated aspects without experiencing a forceful or violent discharge. The awareness of the information revealed in this rhythm, the kind of discharge that may be necessary, or how the body can resolve it without discharge is gained from Stage Five. When we merge with what lies behind the illusion, information is gained on an unconscious level. We become aware of what is behind the illusion and gain a cellular understanding of the nature of the alienated rhythm. When we moved with the rhythm of Stage Five, we acknowledged and reached out to the patterns that had not yet merged with the rest of our bodymind. This process carried us naturally into Stage Six.

A Time for Change

Stage Six provides a timely window of opportunity for us to make needed modifications in our lives in preparation for resolution. It is often a time to change lifestyle habits, open to new perspectives on healing, and commit to wellness. It may be the time when we decide to change from a meat-based to a plant-based diet or increase our intake of more whole and unprocessed foods, for instance.

Stage Six also provides an ideal opportunity to begin an exercise program. Serious long-term commitments to participate in healthy exercise like brisk walking, jogging, aerobics, and swimming often begin as we enter the sixth stage of healing. If we have been given an invitation for a free introductory visit to a gym, or were once presented a gift certificate for a spa treatment, bodywork session, chiropractic adjustment or massage, this stage is often the time when we finally decide to use it. We are open to new alternatives to help facilitate our forward movement into the later stages of healing.

Stage Six was especially important to Sarah, the woman who underwent two angioplasties. After moving through Stage Five, when she was forced to challenge her distorted self-images, Sarah decided to adopt two major lifestyle changes that are typical of the early phases of Stage Six: she chose to eliminate most of the fat from her diet and decided to take a brisk one-hour walk each day.

Changing her diet took some work, but after a few weeks Sarah discovered that eating for health could also be eating for pleasure. It soon became a daily adventure to recreate her favorite recipes and develop new ones. She and her family began looking forward to her low-fat creations.

Because it was a natural expression of her ongoing healing process, brisk walking was not the chore Sarah once imagined it to be. She began walking with her neighbors around a nearby track. Although she had to gradually work up to her one-hour goal, her walks became an essential part of her daily routine, and she expanded her range to include different routes around the neighborhood. After three months, Sarah consulted her cardiologist, who had supported her in her healing process. He was pleased that she had lost twenty pounds, and he reduced her heart medication significantly. When he learned that she had achieved her goal of walking an hour a day he looked her in the eye and said, "Now make it two: an hour in the morning and another after dinner." After a year and a half, Sarah not only lost sixty pounds, but also experienced increased energy and stamina.

Stage Six is also a good time to begin activities like meditation, biofeedback, and yoga. In Stage Six, we become involved in these practices not so much for therapeutic reasons, but primarily to improve bodymind functions. We naturally gravitate toward activities that improve our capacity for movement and awareness, which, in turn, enhance our capacity for growth and needed change.

Our passage through Stage Six can be both exciting and purposeful. Although we may not achieve dramatic flashes of enlightenment where we suddenly have the answers to all of our problems, the self-improvement programs that we may not have been ready to hear about before, now become a natural, commonsense alternative. As a result, we naturally move into new activities which bring us a great deal of pleasure.

Serendipity

To many, Stage Six often appears magical because it is the stage when serendipity (the natural talent that some people have for finding interesting or valuable things "by chance") begins to appear. It is not that serendipity never existed, but now the bodymind is both open and flexible enough to accommodate it. The following examples illustrate how serendipity can occur in Stage Six.

When William moved out of Stage Five into the early part of Stage Six, he decided to change his diet. Later that afternoon, one of his co-workers showed him a book on vegetarian cooking. He later told me, "That is strange . . . this was exactly what I was looking for!"

After Elizabeth entered Stage Six, she began thinking about going to a bodyworker. On her birthday a friend gave her a gift certificate for a shiatsu massage at the local wellness center.

For months, Carla wanted to visit a chiropractor, but she had no idea whom to see. One day her cousin, whom she hadn't seen for a year, phoned to suggest she go to his chiropractor.

In the early part of Stage Six, opportunities that are in alignment with our betterment often appear unexpectedly because we are now more receptive to them. It may seem these events happen as if by coincidence, and as a result we are often pleasantly surprised. We may say, "Look what happened today — can you believe it? I was thinking of taking up jogging, and my brother gave me a new pair of running shoes!" This type of experience is common in the early part of Stage Six. Each time serendipity comes into our lives, we are surprised. Even when it happens several times in one day we may remark, "Hmm. This is strange!"

Cause or Effect?

As Stage Six progresses, we become more energized and more flexible on all levels, which produces a greater level of body tension in preparation for Stage Seven, Resolution. Often it is difficult to determine if the readiness to resolve in Stage Six occurs because we moved into the consciousness of Stage Six or because of the new

programs we are using, like diet and exercise. It doesn't really matter. In earlier stages we may have changed our diets or adopted other
practices for self-improvement, but may not have experienced the
chemical changes (such as detoxification) we expected. But when
we get to the sixth stage of healing, we automatically become open
to letting go of what we could not previously release.

Richard's Stage Six experience involved relinquishing old eating
habits and letting go of excess weight:

> I have always eaten things that have made me feel very
> sick and brought on asthma. Wheat, big meals, a lot of
> food, and anything and everything I could stuff down
> my throat. Now, I know what not to touch and eat. The
> miracle is that I don't do it anymore . . . . And aside from
> [not triggering my asthma by poor eating habits], I've
> lost ten pounds.

Like the earlier stages, we do not need to know why we are
becoming more flexible during Stage Six. And most of us don't know
why, which is actually fortunate, because when we are conscious of
why we are changing, we often sabotage our movements by becoming preoccupied with the process, feeling confused about where it
may be taking us, or doubting the inherent wisdom and perfection
involved. When this takes place, we are often thrown into the earlier stages of healing.

Moving Through Stage Six

Stanley often suffered from abdominal cramps. Whenever he
experienced them, he found himself leaning forward and running his
hands in a circular motion down his thighs, as if he were pushing
his energy down toward his knees. At the same time he involuntar-
ily rocked back and forth, grunting and breathing through his nose.
He somehow got into a rhythm with the cramps and soon after
found that he was moving his bowels with great relief.

When Mary became very angry or upset, she would sit in a chair, tap her right foot, and breathe strongly through her nose. She would also swirl her hands in a circular motion on the top of her head, periodically pausing to grab her hair. Afterward her anger would dissipate on its own or she would automatically yell or scream and her tension would release.

We often observe babies and small children rubbing their eyes in a circular motion as they prepare to cry. Sometimes the tears do not appear after this motion.

As mentioned earlier, when we move further through Stage Six, we often experience the feeling of impending release. It is not unlike the feeling we have when we are about to throw up or have to sneeze. For others, it may be an awareness that they need to let out a scream or shed some tears. We may have the feeling that something is going to have to change in our relationship or that we will soon decide to end a long pattern of addiction. A later phase of Stage Six often brings up uncomfortable feelings. They manifest as tension builds in the bodymind while it gets ready to discharge the rhythm, pattern, information, or energy that no longer works for us and is not in harmony with the rest of our bodymind's rhythm.

Aborting the Process

Because it can be uncomfortable, the later part of Stage Six is when many individuals attempt to modify or abort it. For example, when we feel we are going to throw up, we may reach for anti-nausea medication. We may experience emotional anxiety when we feel we are about to yell or scream, and we take a tranquilizer or see a psychiatrist to feel more comfortable.

In Stage Six, it is imperative — providing we have gone through the previous stages — that we consult the kind of healing practitioner who does not automatically treat symptoms so that we become comfortable. Stage Six calls for a practitioner who can, when needed, support us in further movement into chaos, an essential feature of Stage Seven.

Remember, impending chaos is not to be feared. Although it often involves moving beyond our comfort range, chaos is absolutely essential for meaningful change and healing to take place. Chaos offers us the opportunity to redirect our lives in harmony with the new understandings and new perspectives we have gained in our journey through the earlier stages, and it can be a welcome step in the adventure we call transformation.

Although the feelings involved in a buildup of tension may be uncomfortable, if we have successfully moved through the previous stages, we know this tension and discomfort is somehow OK. However, if we feel uncomfortable in Stage Six and have not had support from others to help us move through it, we may decide that something is wrong and choose to stop the process. During this stage it is common for people to drink alcohol or take drugs to avoid the discomfort.

In a true Stage Six consciousness (after successfully learning the rhythms of stages One through Five), there is discomfort, tension, anxiety, *and* the feeling that we need to move through it. If we have successfully grown into and through the previous stages, just as we reach for the drink or the drug — or otherwise attempt to inhibit ourselves from fully experiencing this stage of healing, we somehow realize that "This is not what I need." Although we know that something is happening as we move past our comfort zone, we also know that the process is right and that we need to participate in it despite the transitory anxiety, fear, or discomfort.

Moving with the Flow

Connecting with the rhythm of Stage Six will take over our physical and emotional being and will allow us to build up the tension necessary for the resolution that occurs in Stage Seven. We need to build momentum before reaching Stage Seven, but again, our experience in Stage Six need not be uncomfortable. At a point during lovemaking, we know that an orgasm is coming. The feeling is one of both high stimulation and increased energy buildup.

Women who have delivered babies through natural childbirth are often aware of the kind of tension that is characteristic of Stage Six. As the baby's head moves through the birth canal, an increase in contractions and breathing occurs. The mother may rub her belly and breathe in a similar way that Stanley and Sarah did. With this rhythm the mother will naturally move toward the moment of birth.

By moving with the natural rhythm of Stage Six, initial feelings of discomfort, fear, or ambivalence are replaced with calm expectation connected to the desire to move on, to release, and to relinquish. Whether it is the release of the bowels associated with cramps, the vomiting necessary when we need to eliminate stomach contents, or the need to scream "Stop. Leave me alone!", we begin to welcome the prospect of discharge.

The later phase of Stage Six can be an exciting and dynamic process. When the rhythm of Stage Six builds, it appears as if all the energy channels of the body are feeding into one greater channel to create the tension necessary for us to move with confidence and eager anticipation into Stage Seven.

As tension builds, it is only the judgment occurring earlier — especially with Stage Two concepts of "good-bad," "right-wrong" — that tends to make us feel, "This is not right." If the discharge process were to occur in Stage Two, for example, we would become very upset and feel that something is really wrong with us, leading us to say, "I have to stop this." But, in Stage Six, we no longer deal with our polarities. Because we have gained experience and wisdom from the earlier stages, we feel more whole, have a greater sense of who we are, and are more in touch with our natural rhythms. We feel confident that the approaching discharge is both timely and appropriate. By the time we complete the sixth stage, our sense of self is more defined and we feel strong enough to move into the next stage of healing.

Seeking Help

I mentioned that Stage Six is a good time to seek health professionals who will help us to further the process of expansion and growth, as opposed to those who seek to control or manage symptoms. Stage Six is the time, for example, when what is known as the "homeopathic constitutional remedy" can be very effective. It is also a time when acupuncture — not for pain relief but for removing the blockage of *qi* energy — produces powerful results.

Bodymind-oriented disciplines like chiropractic, Core Energetics, bioenergetics, Rolfing, Hellerwork, Trager bodywork, and Huna Kane bodywork can be extremely helpful to increase mobility, remove energy blocks, and help build up energy in preparation for resolution. After a session with a good bodywork facilitator, we sometimes move into a chaotic episode, which may be part of the beginning of Stage Seven. However, our intent at this time is not to move out of Stage Six, but to allow the rhythm of this stage to carry us through it, just as if we were to ride an ocean wave onto the shore.

For some people, tension may also build until they experience a stronger sense of self. As a result, no major discharge is necessary. Sometimes the feeling of tension builds and the individual is comfortable with the increased tension. That experience may be enough for the dissonant rhythm or alienated aspect of the bodymind to naturally resolve itself. Discharge, if appropriate, may occur at a later point during the healing journey.

Hearing Yourself Ask for Help

As you gain the momentum for impending resolution and seek methods that will better prepare you for the next stage, you may hear yourself ask something like, "God, please let this new [diet, exercise] help me to change. Please let this [chiropractic, acupuncture, shiatsu] help me overcome my limits."

This prayer may sound like the wishful thinking of Stage Two. However, there is a major difference: you are not asking that these new methods magically resolve your distress. Instead, you have healed sufficiently to ask that these procedures or practitioners help you do your healing.

As the tension builds and you move closer to the end of Stage Six, you may hear yourself say, "God, please give me the strength for what is coming. Give me the strength to make this break-through."

Stage Six Exercise

Lie comfortably on your back. Breathe gently and deeply in and out through your nose. Place your hands above the area where there is tension, and move them in circular motions on the tense region. Synchronize your breathing with your hand movements. Breathe deeply through your nose with each circular motion. Let the rhythm take over. As Stage Six completes, the rhythm of Stage Seven often takes over, sometimes rather dramatically, producing discharge and resolution, as explained in the next chapter.

Stage Six Declarations

"I am flexible."
"I am building momentum."
"I am ready."
"It's OK to let go!"

Stage Six Exercise

7

STAGE SEVEN

Resolution

"The wheel does not break,
'Tis the band round my heart
That, to lessen its ache,
When I grieved for your sake,
I bound round my heart."
But it was the breaking of the other bands from faithful
Henry's heart, because he was so relieved and happy.

— "THE FROG PRINCE"

When my son was in the fourth grade, he announced one morning that he didn't want to go to school because he was sick. I asked him, "What do you mean by sick?" He replied that he had just thrown up his breakfast and was running a fever. Although I decided not to send him to school that day, I began to think, if he was not running a fever and his body was not trying to rid itself of poisons through vomiting, then he would *really* be sick.

What most people consider as sickness is usually the body trying, through discharge, to release something it does not want in order to achieve a new level of health. Successful discharge involves our bodymind's system going from higher tension to lower tension, from a state of distress toward ease. Discharge is a natural, automatic (requiring no conscious thought) process that most people take for granted. Stage Seven resolves the buildup of tension experienced in Stage Six. The result is resolution.

Many of us have felt a good sneeze coming on, but couldn't quite get ourselves to sneeze. Then suddenly it happens: we have a terrific sneeze and it is a tremendous relief! We may have awakened in the middle of the night feeling nauseated, knowing that if only we could vomit we would feel better. After discharge, we feel relaxed and relieved.

We all have experienced a buildup of physical and emotional tension until we cannot tolerate it anymore. Someone or something may upset us and we suddenly express our emotions through screaming or yelling or having a good cry. What a relief it is! Similarly, a feeling of rising tension builds up during lovemaking. Our body may release this tension through a powerful, and pleasurable discharge.

The discharge process can be subtle, such as weeping following a particularly emotional experience, or it can be dramatic. When we sneeze, we exert a force of more than one hundred miles per hour. When the body needs to clean its lower intestinal tract, it can produce a strong bowel movement. Other examples of discharge may be a fit of crying, screaming, or even hitting an object (such as a mattress or a pillow) to release anger, frustration, or other kinds of emotional tension. Discharge can also be expressed as a fit of laughter, a big smile, or a long sigh of relief.

Resolution is the state of consciousness that produces feelings of calm, accomplishment, success, and a sense of freedom and peace. This state implies that integration has occurred between an alienated part of ourself and the rest of us. Our dissonant aspects have had the opportunity to merge with the basic rhythm of wholeness characteristic of Stage Five (Merging). With the information gained in Stage Five, and the momentum built in Stage Six, in Stage Seven we become grounded, flexible, and adaptable enough to release the isolated or "false" aspects of our being.

In Stage Seven, discharge is the means of achieving the state of resolution. When discharge occurs at earlier stages, we often focus on what we have lost, which results in increased tension between our true self and the alienated aspects of our being. For this reason, it is often an unwelcome event involving giving up something that a part of us still needs. In contrast, when discharge occurs in Stage

Seven, our focus is primarily on the wholeness of our being and on eliminating something we no longer need. It is a welcome event that we have expected and prepared ourselves for.

Discharge: A Natural Part of Healing

When the process of discharge occurs, you may say, "I am sick because I have bladder cramps and every few minutes I try to urinate but nothing comes out." The body may be trying to keep the bladder aseptic, which is its natural state. If there is a toxin in the urinary system, the body will filter it through the kidney to the ureters, the tubes that carry urine to the bladder for elimination. In more acute cases, the nervous system may cause a contraction in the bladder so that fluid is eliminated a few drops at a time; in that way the body can continue its self-cleansing operations.

During this process blood may be found in urine. We may decide to consult a physician, because we've been taught that blood in urine means we are sick and that the discharge process has gone "too far." Yet, blood may be found in urine from capillaries that leaked in order to allow more white blood cells to enter the bladder and finish cleaning the debris. Is the body sick, or is it creating a discharge process to maintain a healthy state?

Yes, the discharge process is significant and at times potentially dangerous. And blood in urine may mean that an unhealthy process is occurring. The body has dynamic processes that may express themselves both by becoming ill (because of malfunction) and by becoming healthy (because of improved function). A key factor in this example, as with all others in this chapter, is our internal awareness of alignment (or lack of alignment) with our natural rhythms.

Fever

One way the body creates discharge is through fever. For every degree Fahrenheit the body temperature rises, the heart increases its rate by ten beats a minute and the body increases the urine filtration to better cleanse the system. At the same time, more blood forms to increase carbon dioxide and oxygen exchange and the heart sends this blood to the kidneys for filtration and elimination at a greater rate. The higher metabolic rate in the system enables the body to do two things: it increases the rate of filtration and hastens the process of oxidation, two essential processes for ridding the body of toxins.

When our temperature rises above 98.6, the opportunity for viruses and bacteria to survive in the body decreases. In addition, in this elevated thermal state, our bodies produce larger quantities of interferon (a powerful anti-virus protein) .

Ironically, whenever our temperature rises more than one or two degrees above "normal," we are conditioned to consult a doctor or take a drug designed to lower it. Very few people allow their body temperature to rise naturally to 102 or 103 degrees Fahrenheit (or even higher) without interfering with the natural rhythm of the discharge process.

Whenever we interfere with the process, the result is that we often create more of what our bodies are trying to eliminate. For example, by suppressing the fever, we permit microbes and toxins to proliferate. We have unwittingly assisted in producing a powerful threat to health because we have not resolved the underlying cause of the chaos. Through a successful discharge in Stage Seven, on the other hand, a stronger sense of an integrated "I am" occurs, resulting in a sense of completion or accomplishment.

Healing: An "Out of Control" Response

When we go beyond our usual experiences we may say, "Hey, something's wrong;" "What is it," "How long is it going to last?" or "Someone please help it stop." The "it" we refer to may be a spasm in our backs, a fever, vomiting, or emotional experiences like fear or rage. We have been socialized to believe that "it" is dangerous.

One goal of modern medicine is to control or eliminate all discharge so that patients can be brought back to their "normal" levels of functioning. Therefore, resolution cannot occur. Through medication or other therapeutics, fever is eliminated, the feeling of nausea is decreased, or the headache disappears. We may then feel we are more in control. Consistent with its intent, modern medicine is often effective in this regard. The question is, "What does this have to do with healing?"

Our society supports the control of phenomena like discharge in order to make us feel more comfortable. When we are out of control we are considered "sick" and are advised to seek professional help. Most visit physicians if we have physical problems, and the clergy for psychological, marital, or spiritual problems. Depending on the nature of the difficulty, we may also seek psychotherapists, social workers, or attorneys.

The accepted path of action is to find someone who knows more about the problem and have that person "put things right." Even if we remain beyond control in the discharge process, we often accept it as normal if a professional tells us it is. For example, if we sneeze continuously, we may be afraid that our sneezing is out of control. But if the physician says it's hay fever, it becomes acceptable to sneeze continuously; we are given permission to sneeze because we have hay fever. We feel more in control and therefore no longer fearful of the situation. We are then able to return to the status quo.

In nearly twenty years in the health care field, I have found that healing — as opposed to curing — involves a resolution of dissonant rhythms and the release of trapped energy. Resolution occurs through discharge. "Discharge" literally means "no charge." In other words, discharge refers to the release of energy or tension. Discharge may involve the release of trapped energy, repressed or ignored information, or toxins on physical, emotional, mental, and spiritual levels. Releasing may allow us to access our higher potential and often includes a temporary loss of control.

Despite the fact that the medical community sees being in control as the basis of health, we must realize that we cannot be healthy unless we go out of control, the very process of which enables us to create change in our lives. Healing, therefore, involves being out of control; discharge is an out of control response. We are "out of control" from our norm judged by our educated minds. But being out of control is necessary so that we can reconnect to our internal, infinite healing power.

The Case of Eileen

One of the most dramatic cases of discharge I have seen involves Eileen, a courageous woman. Eileen came to me for chiropractic adjustments several times a week for more than a year. Since childhood her lymphatic system on the left side of her body had been obstructed. When I met her, her left leg had enlarged to several times its normal size. I felt that sooner or later a powerful discharge would take place, although I did not tell Eileen to expect it.

When she visited her mother in Atlanta (also a chiropractor), her leg became even bigger and an infection set in. She could no longer walk and her fever rose to 107 degrees. Doctors recommended immediate amputation so that she could lead a "normal" life.

Eileen refused to undergo surgery. She also rejected antibiotics and pain killers. Eileen was in Stage Six and intuitively felt she did not want to interfere with the process. She had had both drug therapy and surgery, and now chose chiropractic adjustments and the services of a physician who used homeopathy. This was a Stage Six decision.

After several days, her leg became redder and darker and two growths the size of golf balls began to appear: one next to the knee and another above the ankle. Within hours a hole the size of a quarter appeared on the growth next to the knee and large quantities of liquid began to drain. After several hours, her condition stabilized.

During the next several days, the growth above her ankle opened and cupfuls of pus and fluid drained. Her fever fluctuated widely and she slept intermittently through the process. Days later, she walked to an airplane and returned to New York. Over the next several weeks, her leg continued to drain. After a while, both holes closed. Within four weeks, Eileen was wearing shoes of equal size for the first time in seven years and was taking dancing lessons.

Since that episode, Eileen has visited stages One through Seven several times, but has not had the need for another intense episode of discharge. On several occasions she has moved to the higher stages of healing. The moral of the story is that Eileen, by going through her healing "hell," emerged with an absolute trust in the sovereignty of her own healing process.

The Dangers of Discharge

After hearing about this remarkable case, you may wonder if it is ever dangerous not to stop the discharge. A discharge process in a system unable to reset itself can be dangerous because the body is determined to eliminate toxins at whatever the cost. The result may be discharge without resolution. Sometimes it can be fatal.

But remember: It is not the discharge itself that is dangerous. It is the lack of resolution or recovery from the discharge process — the inability of the body to fully discharge the toxic event — that creates the dangerous situation.

There is a distinction between discharge in the resolution stage (Stage Seven) and discharge in the suffering stage (Stage One), even if we experience the same symptoms. In physical or emotional suffering we feel helpless and trapped (Stage One), but are incapable of further initiating the healing process. Medical or other therapeutic intervention may indeed be necessary. In contrast, discharge associated with the healing process in Stage Seven may outwardly appear the same as suffering. However, we have a sense of being an observer to the process rather than a victim.

The discharge process in Stage Seven will take place when the nervous system is flexible enough to recover from it. This contrasts to having symptoms of discharge but feeling something is really wrong, or trapped, or helpless, or that the process must be stopped. These experiences are consistent with the lower stages of healing.

In the following list compare the statements associated with discharge in Stage One versus Stage Seven.

Stage One: Suffering

"I feel like a victim (of this situation or condition)."
"When is it going to stop?"
"Get rid of the pain."
"Why is this happening to me?"
"I feel like I am going to die."
"There is no way out."
"Stop it, just stop it."
"I'll do anything. Someone take this away from me."
"I can't be helped."
"God is betraying me."

Stage Seven: Resolution

"This feels lousy, but I know I have to let it happen."
"I don't feel very well, but I know it's OK."
"What am I going to do about this?"
"How long am I going to let this happen?"
"Do I need to ask for help, or am I OK without it?"
"I'm not sure if this is OK."
"This seems to be working."
"Something is releasing."
"Yuk! This is good."

Medical therapy has few accepted means of determining which discharges are physiologically normal and which are pathological. Fortunately, more physicians are learning about the impact a patient's emotional, mental, and spiritual state can have on their physical condition. Many of today's holistic practitioners understand that the discharge process is not necessarily an indicator of disease, but may be part of a healing crisis involving resolution. Considering that most symptoms are self-limiting, more patients, and certainly more practice members, are learning to let nature take her course.

We have said that the body is greater than the sum of its parts, and that the nervous system expresses an innate intelligence that animates, motivates, heals, coordinates, and inspires all functions. From this perspective, there can be no health without resolving our lack of wholeness, which often involves an overt discharge. In other words, lack of *needed* discharge equals lack of health.

Discharge: A Call to Change

For some people discharge is a massive awakening to create change: it is the way their bodies alert them that change is both imminent and necessary. As German psychologist Thorwald Dethlefsen wrote in *The Healing Power of Illness*,

> That which constantly reveals itself as a series of bodily symptoms is the visible expression of an invisible process; it is designed as a signal whose function is to stop us in our tracks, reveal that something is no longer in order, and make us ask questions about what lies behind it all.

For example, we experience abdominal cramps and find that our body is eliminating its intestinal contents. Our body's intelligence is saying "I am eliminating something from the intestinal tract. I need help, love, and attention." When we can see this perspective, we may become more cautious about what we put into our body or how we handle stress. And we can use this knowledge to honor our bodymind which is trying to eliminate what no longer serves it.

Another example is the common nosebleed. Sometimes, a nosebleed may be caused by high blood pressure. But usually high blood pressure is artificially reduced without taking a serious look at the factors within the individual as a whole which created the hypertensive state. Tension is often the result of unresolved feelings or information that is accumulating in the bodymind and is not being processed. It resembles the tension of a coiled spring. Artificially reducing blood pressure may be an effective temporary measure, but a far more important concern is that the spring may still be dangerously coiled under tension.

Discharge: An Intelligent Response

Any aspect of our "self" that no longer works for our healing will be discharged by our innate intelligence. If we are attached to eating a particular food, such as hamburger, and our bodymind does not want high animal fat content, we may have cramps or diarrhea. Then, if we make changes in our diet, we may find that the discharge process intensifies as our bodymind further eliminates those elements that no longer work for its benefit. We may want to eat different foods; the urge for foods that we once enjoyed may decrease or even disappear when we move into the next stage of healing.

The bodymind may want to eliminate anything (food, lifestyle, habit) that no longer serves its highest good, including smoking, drinking, or arguing. For some, this may be a time to change careers, end certain relationships, and even give away what were once prized possessions. Some relinquishments may appear to be involuntary: the car is totaled, partners leave us, or we suddenly lose a lot of money in the stock market.

Many people will ask, "How can you say that someone destroying my car, taking my partner, or going bankrupt can be created by my infinite intelligence preparing to heal me?" In Stage One (Suffering), there is no way we can see the connection, because the consciousness of suffering has limits that do not include observing our process. But when we are healed enough for these events to occur through the discharge process of Stage Seven, we can begin to see the connection.

If the loss of a relationship with a partner, car, or bank account initiates headaches, backaches, high blood pressure, or other conditions, then we have "told" our bodymind that this possession is indeed perceived as a part of who we are. Rather than think it strange that our higher intelligence could somehow seek to change or relinquish our attachment to our possessions, consider this: Isn't it strange that if we lose a physical possession illness could result? How is it possible that we could have developed so much attachment to a car, a partner, or money that we give more power to them than to our healing process? If we don't think this has happened, then why is it that so many of us suffer when we lose these possessions?

At some stage your infinite intelligence may have no option other than to relinquish such a relationship. The result may be its total discharge in order to promote the further expression of the real you.

Relinquishing the Self

In Chapter One, I mentioned that the self is the essential part of our nature that makes us different from everyone else. As we progress through stages One through Six, we begin to achieve a deeper sense of self and the strength that naturally comes about from a greater degree of selfhood.

One concept inherent in the twelve stages of healing is a temporary or functional change in our sense of self necessary for healing to occur. If our stomach modifies its sense of self and discards what no longer works for it, we may have pain, vomiting, or diarrhea. An altered sense of self in our heart may manifest as a changing heart rhythm. And a loss of our existing sense of self may lead us to give up possessions we identified with as a part of our being.

The discharge process involves the bodymind ridding itself of those aspects of self (applied to the personality level and to each body cell) that no longer work for its highest good. It involves discharging the rhythm that cannot live in harmony with the whole. So, what we call "sick" and what we call "well" must undergo considerable modifications. For example, if you are sneezing and someone says, "Oh, you have a cold," you needn't agree but can reply, "My body is discharging." If you are running a fever, instead of thinking, "I must be sick," think, "My body is cleansing." These responses acknowledge your body's intelligence, as well as your taking responsibility for your health. They show that you understand what is happening, as opposed to being a victim of forces over which you have no control.

Judgment

When you refer to "my arm," "my shoulder," or "my leg," your bodymind identifies that body part as being an extension of yourself. When you feel pain or discomfort, or when an organ goes through a discharge, you may become judgmental about it, a common event in Stage Two.

J. Krishnamurti, the Indian philosopher, often said that to help someone with a problem, all you had to do was understand it without judgment and see it clearly; in time this understanding will be transmitted to the person with the problem. The same holds true when a part of your body — a part of your being — experiences a problem or symptom.

Because of judgment, people often set limits on how far they are willing to go with their discharge. When this occurs, discharge is most likely taking place in an early healing stage. Our desire for comfort during discharge limits our healing. By contrast, when we surrender to the process of being out of control, a deeper spiritual awareness can occur. In that process of surrender, we relinquish judgment and increase trust in our infinite wisdom as part of the wisdom of the universe. Healing is now able to develop.

Our movement through the rhythms of the previous six stages teaches us to trust in the process. This implies naturally relinquishing the judgment that it is wrong or right to discharge. After we have achieved resolution, we may become aware of what changes we may need to make so that our body can move ahead to a new state of awareness and peace when we enter Stage Eight.

Going Back into the Closet (and Cleaning It Out)

Achieving the seventh stage implies that we have rid ourselves of old experiences, information, and other excess baggage. This process can be compared to cleaning out our closet.

Imagine that one afternoon you go into your room (which can represent yourself) and decide to clean out your closet, (which can represent any part of your bodymind). Over the years, you have put many memories from past experiences into this closet. Some are in photo albums and are pictures of relationships and events that took place during your childhood. Some are boxes filled with private letters. You may find diaries, locked for years, that contain not only sad thoughts and unrealized hopes, but also pressed flowers or favors from a prom. You may find stuffed animals, old candy bars, or pieces of food that you put in a jacket pocket.

Even though you realize there is much work to be done, you begin cleaning. You reach in and pull out one item, but this may start an avalanche of other items as well and produce a flood of memories (and symptoms).

The same thing happens when we engage in the process of self-discovery and healing. The old food may fall out of the jacket pocket and trigger a cellular memory that may result in, for example, diarrhea, as the body eliminates the toxic material it has become reacquainted with. We may look at photo albums and see images we may have pushed to the backs of our minds. This may cause tension or discharge in the parts of our bodies that are connected to these old images. As a chiropractor, I have found that many old patterns in "the backs of our minds" are often impressed upon different areas of the spine, producing interference and tension in the nervous and muscular systems. My perception is that the spine is indeed the "back of the mind." Therefore, interference in the spine may manifest as many symptoms, including pain.

You may laugh or cry as you walk down Memory Lane. A box may represent a car accident that affected your neck; an old album may symbolize a divorce. The old food may represent a distasteful business partnership. As you continue, you realize you are ready to look at the aspects of your past you had avoided and are now prepared to release. As the energetic bonds to these items are released, you no longer need the items in your closet. You realize they are just cluttering up space. This is similar to what your innate intelligence does when it takes you into the resolution process through discharge.

However, let us imagine that a member of our family, a friend, or our physician walks into the room and declares, "Your room is more of a mess than ever. Why did you create so much trouble for yourself? Just put everything back into the closet." You may reply, "Listen, this may seem chaotic and messy to you and the discharge of what I am throwing away may not make you comfortable. You may see me laugh or cry or throw up as my body goes down Memory Lane. But I am OK with it!" This statement is characteristic of Stage Seven, Resolution.

In the discharge process, we have chosen to clean out our closets. As a result of healing we have already done in stages One through Six, we are now able to spontaneously release what no longer serves us, without the need for additional conscious effort on our part. As this occurs, we may again merge with our suffering as we experience images and items from our past, yet now we recognize that they are only events we have already passed through. We realize that the past is only as powerful as we want it to be, because now we know that the only important time is the present.

The rhythm of the stage of resolution now takes over and we go through the point of discharge, which is necessary to help us throw out those things we no longer need. What happens is that we have more room (a more flexible system) to store more material, more information, and fresh life experiences that are not extensions of the past, thereby creating a fuller experience of the present moment.

Attitudes in Discharge, but not in Resolution

Five major attitudes may appear during the discharge process that are often connected to old patterns now being released. They are not associated with the resolution, but because we are discussing discharge, it is the appropriate time to understand the difference between the process of discharge compared to the consciousness of the resolution stage. If you experience any of the following attitudes for more than brief moments, your discharge process is probably occurring in a stage other than Stage Seven. These attitudes may appear at many stages, yet they are more obvious or apparent in Stage Seven.

1. *Fear* is perhaps the most common distracting attitude brought up by the discharge process. We may have fear of losing control, fear of change, fear of the future, fear that we have a serious illness, or even fear of death. When we have moved through the stages of healing in sequence, fear rarely comes up during resolution. But when the process is out of sync, the lack of nervous system flexibility can bring up feelings of fear. In addition, we must be careful not to take on the fear of others who may feel uncomfortable with our discharge process.

2. *Resentment* can be directed toward ourselves, family members, or others who may be connected to the emotions we have kept inside and are now releasing. Often, feelings of self-resentment can sabotage the healing process; we subconsciously want to punish ourselves or hurt our chances for success.

3. *Personal violation* is often felt when we imagine ourselves to be victims of the discharge process. We ask ourselves, "Why me?" We may be angry at ourselves, at God, and at the world, or we may direct anger toward people who are trying to assist us in the healing process, like our friends, relatives, or health care facilitator. When we feel violated, we often distract ourselves from the process of healing. Expressing the emotions behind the violation is essential,

and the nervous system is more able to deal with the anger brought about by entering this healing stage. Observing the emotion, compared to experiencing violation (Stage One, Suffering), comes about naturally as part of Stage Seven.

4. *Loneliness* is a common feeling while in the process of transformation. It often occurs during discharge. Taking responsibility for our health involves making decisions, which can make us feel alone. Loneliness is often a product of an old sense of self that believes we (as well as our struggles) are separate from others. As a result of this belief, we tend not to reach out to others and ask for their comfort, understanding, and support.

5. *Guilt* is the unhappy feeling that we did something wrong or failed to do something we should have done. Guilt involves experiencing a loss of the moment here and now and is associated with self-judgment and self-punishment. Many of us have carried the burden of guilt since childhood. Guilt says no to the forward movement of life and is associated with an armoring of both the nervous system and the muscular system. It prevents us from experiencing life at this moment and inhibits our forward momentum during the healing process.

When any of these attitudes arise, we often become stuck. We may feel angry and decide that the healing process doesn't work because the situation appears to be getting worse. We may look outside for the answer and go to a physician, chiropractor, or psychotherapist to help us. We may judge ourselves as failures for being afraid or for not trusting our process. We may give up on ourselves and perpetuate a sustaining cycle of low self-esteem.

However, we can move through the physical illness at its acute stage and the distracting attitudes that accompany it, be they (1) fear, (2) resentment, (3) violation, (4) loneliness, or (5) guilt. We can deal with whatever surfaces at the moment. Our experience of discharge makes us aware that we are involved in a process that is not the result of conscious thought. It may even seem strange that we "feel OK with it." We do not have to cultivate patience, forgiveness, or acceptance of our reality. All we need is to be aware of the process. The power that is You is totally in control while the personal you is out of control. And for many of us, it is time this happened!

Walking in the woods, working in the garden, listening to healing sounds, meditating, and praying are often useful during this important stage of healing. However, many activities we once thought would facilitate healing may not work for us while things we did not think were healing do. Rather than sit quietly by a babbling brook or meditating under a tree, we may prefer to participate in a marching band or attend a rock concert. We can acknowledge that certain experiences may now affect us differently than they did before we entered this stage of healing.

Seeking Help

It is always advisable to seek help when you feel the need. The more you heal, the more you will be sensitive to whether or not you need help. And the further along the stages you go, the easier it will be to ask for it. Any vehicle that helps you better honor yourself with gratitude is always beneficial.

People often seek treatment, including antibiotics, antihistamines, ultrasound, tranquilizers, manipulation, and psychotherapy, to make them more comfortable and more in control of their situations during discharge. These therapies may indeed make them more comfortable, or may even prolong life.

During discharge we can choose a healing system that will help us move forward in the journey. Modalities like craniosacral therapy, bioenergetics, Core Energetics, breathwork, sound or tone work, or Zero Balancing assist resolution. Specific chiropractic adjustments are also useful. They release interference within the nervous system so that the bodymind can perceive, adapt to, and recover from unneeded information and move into the discharge process appropriately.

We can heal even if we do not observe discharge. The point of this chapter is to experience the consciousness that will support our necessary resolution. This helps us better appreciate the inner wisdom that expresses itself when discharge occurs naturally and at the appropriate time, without interference.

When it does occur, we may choose homeopathy, acupuncture, herbs, or massage, not to treat the discomfort, but to allow the discharge process to occur (or continue to occur) if our innate wisdom needs it to continue. These systems may also be used to find out where basic blockages are in the bodymind. According to Fritz Frederick Smith, M.D., the developer of Zero Balancing, a structural acupressure system,

> In a healing crisis, ideally we do not treat the symptom; rather we let it run its course. But if the person must have assistance or treatment, the aim is to move forward *through* the problem and not eradicate its symptom per se. The problem should be understood in its proper context in the healing crisis.

If your inner voice says you should go through a therapeutic intervention, by all means do it. But don't confuse treatment or cure with healing. As long as therapeutic intervention is not the general trend and you are in rhythm with the twelve stages of healing, you will continue to move through whatever experiences are necessary to move one step further. Eventually, you will undergo the process of discharge in whatever area must be healed.

The resolution through discharge process does not need to take a long time. If the nervous system is flexible and is kept free of interference, or if there is no adverse tension between the brain and spinal cord, you may move through the process in minutes. If you must develop better communication between your innate intelligence and your educated self (which usually means removing blockages from the nervous system), the process may take longer because your body has more to discharge.

Hearing Yourself Ask for Help

You may hear yourself pray or ask for help with words such as, "Oh God, please make this be easy. Please let me get through this. Make this be worth it. Let this be over soon! I know I need this, but isn't there an easier way?"

Stage Seven Exercises

Standing, sitting, or lying down comfortably, breathe in through your nose and hold it for a moment. Squeeze the breath into your abdomen by contracting your abdominal muscles. Now slowly, and with cheeks puffed out, exhale the breath rhythmically, letting out a little air at a time, yet with a strong final exhale. Repeat.

Close your hands into fists, bend your arms over your head (as if you were doing curls with a barbell) and forcibly bring your arms, then your hands to your thighs as if you were punching them.

If it feels more appropriate to stand, bring your arms over your head, make fists, and forcibly bring your arms down and back, as if you were engaged in downhill skiing. Shouting, crying, or laughing are common as the body integrates with the breath at this stage.

Stage Seven Declarations

"I Am."

"I release that which no longer serves me."

"I come to resolution."

"Oooh," "ahhh," "whooosh." (Natural, instinctive, nonverbal expressions of release that push energy out are appropriate. Allow the rhythm inherent in these sounds to overtake you.)

Stage Seven Exercise

8

STAGE EIGHT

Emptiness in Connectedness

I experience the fullness of my emptiness.

S tage Eight is the stage of emptiness, vulnerability, and possibilities. Emptiness is the portal that leads us to higher states of awareness. It is the door between our usual, customary state of feeling and the states of consciousness in which we are more aware of our wholeness and experience our connectedness with the world around us.

After the discharge of Stage Seven, the emptiness in Stage Eight may be similar to the empty feeling we experience after a powerful bowel movement or the release of a full bladder. It can be the calm and lightness one feels after an orgasm or the feeling of respite after having a fever. It may also be the feeling of aloneness experienced following the loss of a loved one or after leaving a job.

The feelings of emptiness, calmness, and aloneness may seem uncomfortable at first, but they set the stage for deeper exploration and movement. It is as if the dissonant sounds of a construction crew working outside our home for several months have become our daily companion. In Stage Seven, the construction crew completed its job and went home. Now, there is an almost deafening silence. It may be unsettling, because our most valuable inner companions (our basic insights and rhythms) can finally be heard.

Marc Allen, in his book *Tantra for the West*, wrote, "To be alone is to tune into the sacred being of yourself." The beginning phase of Stage Eight provides us with this opportunity.

In Stage Seven, we released much of our "armor" or distraction from our internal natural wholeness. Now, as we emerge from Stage Seven, the stage of Resolution, we may feel raw or vulnerable without the support of some of our usual reference points. Because those aspects of ourselves with which we have identified (or that have been our "companions") are now discharged, we may feel like strangers in a new land. We may feel lonely as we enter this new stage, but our emptiness creates room for new possibilities and connections. It is as if for years we have been carrying, in both arms, whatever it was we just released. While our arms were occupied we were closed off from reaching out for new friends and experiences. Now that our arms are wide open, we feel somewhat unprotected, yet relieved that our burden has been relinquished. We are eager for what awaits us. In *The Keepers of the Earth*, poet Kristin Zambucka writes,

> And as you reach new plateaux of thought . . .
> And old friends drop away,
> Fear not loneliness.
> For there is a silent communication between those at the
> same level of awareness.
> And for the first time you will not be lonely . . .

The essence of Stage Eight is reflected in the symbolism of the biblical story about the Prodigal Son, the youngest son of a rich man. One day the son asked his father to divide the family property. Then he took his share of the fortune and spent it wildly in a faraway land. Within a short time he ran out of money and desperately looked for a job to sustain him. After a while he found a lowly job feeding pigs.

He was poor, hungry, and lonely. In his emptiness he realized the error of his ways and decided to "return home" to ask forgiveness from his father. To his surprise, his father welcomed him with open arms. By experiencing emptiness, the son became open to his inner rhythms, which brought him "home." In the words of his father, "He was dead and has been brought back to life."

The Transition Zone

Emptiness is often confused with nothingness or nonexistence, although it is much more than that. To illustrate the concept of emptiness, let's pretend we are a trapeze artist in the circus. As we let go of one of the trapeze bars, which is similar to letting go or discharging in Stage Seven (Resolution), the other bars represent opportunities that may become our reality if we grab onto them. But as we begin Stage Eight, we have not yet grabbed onto the next bar. The space in between the bars may be called emptiness, the place from where our next bar materializes. It serves as the space of transition from one bar to the other.

Danaan Perry, founder of the Earthstewards Network, referred to this image in *The Essene Book of Days*: "I have a sneaking suspicion that the transition zone is the only real thing, and the bars are illusions we dream up to avoid the void where the real change, the real growth occurs for us."

Many people believe that emptiness is a lifeless void of nothingness that leads to emotional or mental paralysis. However, emptiness, when timed correctly in the healing process, leads to freedom rather than to limitation, because it means we have not *attached our conscious reality to one particular perspective*. Again, it is a place in which we have not yet grabbed a particular trapeze bar to the exclusion of all others. But we will know when it is time to grab onto the next bar. Our inner voice says, "Grab it. Grab it now!" It is louder, stronger, more sure, and easier to follow without the interfering static just released in Stage Seven.

Emptiness is not unlike the figure zero (0). When we contemplate a zero, we can say that it contains nothing; it is empty. Yet, a zero placed after a one (10) or two zeros placed after a one (100) create a different meaning than the number one by itself. In this example, the zero (the nothingness or the emptiness) defines and holds the space for whatever it is associated with. It is six zeros after a one that makes us a millionaire.

It is the emptiness of this page that allows us to see the letters that appear. It is the emptiness around the objects on a painter's canvas that allows us to discern the landscape. It is the emptiness between the notes that allows us to define the music. It is the emptiness of the sky that defines the horizon.

Years ago, one of my college professors taught me a simple concept: "Create an emptiness and it shall be filled." He believed that by creating emptiness, we form a kind of vacuum that attracts people, objects, and experiences to us. After I opened my chiropractic office, I tested this idea. I began taking ten percent of my income and putting it into a special tithing account. Then I would take the money from this account and distribute it to my favorite charities.

By putting money in my tithing account I was creating a space of relative emptiness in my regular bank account. Yet I was pleasantly surprised to find that my income always grew to exceed the amount in my tithing account. Somehow, the more I put in my tithing account, the more life provided me. During those months that I did not make deposits in the tithing account, additional income did not come my way, while additional expenses usually surfaced.

Nature abhors a vacuum and will always seek to fill it. At this stage of the healing process, the vacuum created by emptiness provides the opportunities we need for our continued growth and healing. And when we are filled from our state of emptiness, we are also filled with gratitude.

The Dynamic State of Readiness

Emptiness is a unique state of being that comprises both stillness and tremendous activity. For this reason, I view emptiness as a dynamic state of readiness in which we are poised to move on to discover new realities.

Findings from modern physics state that there is a Primary Space or void from which all matter springs. In other words, it is emptiness from which all is created. In *Beyond the Quantum*, Michael Talbot writes,

> Many physicists believe that at its ultramicroscopic level, empty space is really a turbulent and frothy storm of activity. Moreover, it is now accepted by science that in these violent upheavals in the nothingness, new particles are constantly being created and destroyed. . . . Indeed, a growing number of physicists are coming to believe that everything we know as real in the entire universe may ultimately have sprung out of this empty but seething vacuum.

Let us imagine we have a television set that can pick up a variety of stations. We know that television waves travel through space, but we cannot perceive them. Our senses cannot tune to their frequencies until they are expressed through the proper medium, which is the television set. Therefore, although the waves already exist for us to perceive all the channels, a state of emptiness (relative to our awareness) exists until we turn our set on and tune into a particular channel. So, rather than being a state of nothingness, the emptiness of a blank television screen is actually a state of readiness to receive what is already there.

The same principle can be applied to our perception of new realities when we are in a state of emptiness. All potential realities exist in a field of emptiness, which really is a state of "everything-ness" that cannot be perceived. This field of emptiness is like a holding bin for all possible realities that exist at once. But, because our nervous system can only perceive a limited number of these at one time, the vast field of realities seems empty — like television waves without a set to receive them.

The Status Report

After moving into Stage Eight, we ask our bodymind for a status report so we can find out what it is experiencing. In Stage Eight, we ask, "What do you feel? What is going on?" We may silently ask, "Stomach, what do you feel after the release of stomach contents?" "Chest, what do you feel after coughing?" "Heart center, what do you feel after crying over the break-up of this relationship?"

There is a difference, however, between the internal scan that occurs in Stage Five (Merging) and the one that occurs in Stage Eight (Emptiness). In Stage Five, we look at the area underlying our distress, much like the mythical character who has to return to the lion's den, or the fairy tale hero who finally has to confront the evil giant. By the time we reach Stage Eight, we have gained a sense of merging along with a strength of self and a high degree of internal awareness and wholeness. The feeling of wholeness combined with our emptiness is very powerful. Rather than putting our focus on the pain, distress, or separateness, we pay attention to the emptiness around the area where our recent discharge occurred.

This is like removing a painful splinter from your hand. Because the splinter is causing you pain, your focus is on the splinter as you try to locate it and extract it. When it is finally removed (or resolved in Stage Seven), your perspective expands. Instead of focusing on the small area of distress (the splinter), you now gain a larger perspective. As a result, you experience a feeling of stillness, and from this place you are more receptive to your inner voice. Now you are more aware of wholeness from the area that was numbed or distracted by the attachment to whatever was discharged. Now you are no longer directed by the illusory self and you can hear the chorus of your deeper reality more clearly and fully. This is the Stage Eight experience.

In this stage of healing, your bodymind responds, "This is OK. Somehow I asked for this new state of being." Rather than move away from this new connection with your bodymind, the rhythm of Stage Eight offers you the opportunity to remain with it for a while. As in all stages of healing, connecting with the rhythm of Stage Eight and learning its lessons are very important.

Flowing with Stage Eight

"Row, row, row your boat, gently down the stream. Merrily, merrily, merrily, merrily, life is but a dream." We all know this simple rhyme, but few of us really understand its hidden meaning and how it can help us move through Stage Eight.

The boat represents our physical body, which each of us rows gently down the stream of life. It is an activity done in the stillness of our self and the stream. The song asks us to go "merrily, merrily, merrily, merrily." When we are merry, we open ourselves to the fun and adventure of this journey. Because "life is but a dream," we create from our emptiness whatever we put our focus on — consciously or unconsciously. Our life is a creation of our dreams and we live to express our full potential.

When we row "gently down the stream" of Stage Eight, we can open ourselves to different kinds of internal dialogues, which often take the form of chaotic, yet informative streams of consciousness:

— Somehow this feels lonely. I can feel my digestive system pulsating. I can experience my chest rising and falling where there was congestion before.

— I sense my desire to reach out to her. She is not there, but I still want to reach out.

— I sense a flexibility in my lower back where it used to hurt so much. I can actually feel it move.

— I feel connected to those parts of my being where a connection was missing.

—With the energy I have just released, I somehow feel vulnerable and tender. I sense an internal rhythm very loudly and the rest of my body is actually having a talk with that rhythm. I can sense my heart and my lungs communicating with me.

In Stage Eight, there is an awareness of connections among parts of yourself that formerly had not been connected. After an orgasm, for example, the status report may manifest as a flow of energy moving from your feet up your spine until it radiates throughout your body. Your lover may touch your chest, shoulder, or lip and you may shudder, because your body is now very sensitive and the different parts of your bodymind are communicating without the interference that existed before. The newly freed aspects of your bodymind are telling you, "Thank you for letting go of what blocked my perspective. Pay attention to the wholeness of me."

In Stage Eight, we can sense communication taking place between the new vulnerable areas and the strong, supportive rest of us. We know that something deep within us "knows." We may not yet know what it is, but *we know that we know* and that we will become aware of it soon. Somehow this newness is exciting, yet scary. We may say to ourselves, "Can I be quiet? Can I be still? I experience, I hear, I sense. Am I paying attention to myself?" As we do this, we move with the rhythmic flow of Stage Eight.

Emptiness Without Self-Tyranny

Emptiness is a primary goal of many spiritual seekers and is achieved by different means. Often, it is sought through denial. In many parts of Asia, and in India in particular, aspirants to the spiritual life often perform many ascetic practices to deprive themselves of material things. Some fast for long periods, retreat to monasteries, or go to the desert for extended periods of solitude and meditation. Many become celibate or give up careers, families, and material wealth.

The lives of Jesus, the Buddha, and holy people like Saint Francis, Saint Theresa, and Gandhi all reflect the belief that the path to spiritual union is one of relinquishment of material things. Jesus taught that a camel could go through the eye of a needle more easily than a rich man with many possessions can enter the Kingdom of Heaven. Perhaps the most extreme example of this tradition is a small group of Jain monks, who aspire to a life of *ahimsa* or harmlessness. Not only do the monks embrace poverty, celibacy, and nonviolence, but they refuse to own (or wear) clothes. In some cities in India, they walk through the streets, totally naked, receiving occasional meals from lay members of the Jain religion. In some religious orders, priests and nuns flagellate their bodies to kill desire. Some Indian *saddhus* or holy men go without food and water for weeks in order to subjugate their body and its desire to do the bidding of their spiritual nature.

However, starving oneself and tyrannizing the body does not free the spirit, but instead dishonors it. Our body is not separate from God or the human spirit, but is rather a reflection or expression of the divine. In one of her Guide Lectures, Eva Pierrakos said, "Your spiritual self cannot be freed unless you learn to feel all your feelings, unless you learn to accept every part of your being no matter how destructive it may be right now." As a divine creation, our body deserves honor and respect rather than abuse. Honoring our inner essence and its outward expression is essential for true healing to occur.

There are other ways to achieve a state of emptiness rather than by forcing ourselves to rip away our attachments through tyranny or repression. In the previous stages of healing, we discovered that life will do that for us. Being in our natural flow will create resolution through discharge in Stage Seven, leading to the emptiness of Stage Eight. If we follow our natural rhythms inherent in the different healing stages, whatever we no longer need will gently fall away, melting like the winter's snow under the sun on a warm spring day, or falling like an avalanche.

Counting Our Blessings

Although all stages of healing offer many blessings, those discovered in Stage Eight are usually more pleasurable than the blessings found in the earlier stages of healing. This stage provides us with the opportunity to truly embrace our higher nature and nurture ourselves without reservation.

As we enter Stage Eight, we are likely to feel physically and emotionally vulnerable. For this reason, it is not a time to subject ourselves to lots of extraneous or loud stimulation. Stage Eight offers the opportunity to honor the stillness, the sensitivity, and the subtle rhythms that are connecting within. This is the stage when we are more likely to have a transcendental experience. We will more likely develop a higher state of consciousness, firmly grounded in the strength and stability gained from the lessons learned in the previous stages.

Stage Eight also provides us with the leap of faith we need to follow the rhythms within. This, in turn, guides us to our next stage of healing. (In fact, if we avoid or deny the reality of these rhythms, our bodymind may perceive this as a great violation of our essence.) The decisions we haven't made, or the insights we haven't been cognizant of, begin to occur in this stage. They come about on their own, without effort on our part. Like the trapeze artist reaching for the next bar, we "know" that our awareness is correct. It is a deeper level of knowing than we have ever experienced before.

Maximizing the Stage Eight Experience

While I am not endorsing a particular religious or spiritual path, there are a number of simple practices that can tremendously enhance your movement through Stage Eight.

Religious Teachings. Although religious devotion can be used as a way to avoid suffering in the earlier healing stages, connecting to spiritual and religious teachings in Stage Eight can be very beneficial for healing. It is especially true during holy day periods like Christmas, Easter, Ramadan, the Wesak festival, and Yom Kippur, when spiritual energies are especially strong.

For example, people of Jewish faith are given the opportunity to intensify their spiritual focus during the days between Rosh Hashanah, the Jewish New Year, and Yom Kippur, the Day of Atonement. During this time of reflection, devotion, and asking forgiveness, Jews have the opportunity to experience the first seven stages of healing. They reflect on all their attitudes and actions during the previous year that were out of touch with the rhythms of their true selves or have dishonored others. The time between the two holy days is filled with thoughts especially connected to stages Three, Four, and Five.

On the eve of Rosh Hashanah, they empty themselves of their sins through the symbolic act of casting herbs or flowers upon the water while reciting the prayer "And Thou wilt cast their sins into the depths of the sea" (Micah 7:19). The original meaning of sin is important to understand in the context of healing. The term is derived from "disconnectedness" or "separateness," such as being disconnected from our wholeness or being separated from the Divine. Reciting this prayer is symbolic of discharging our dissonant aspects in Stage Seven.

Jews experience Yom Kippur by preparing for and fasting on the Day of Atonement. A state of emptiness is created that takes them back through stages Six and Seven. And from this state of emptiness (Stage Eight), they can most powerfully ask God for mercy and become open to Divine blessing during the coming year.

Prayer. Praying can be extremely powerful during Stage Eight. Prayer is, in essence, an expression of yearning from the depths of our being to realize our connection to the Source of all life. Prayer acknowledges our union with God. When we pray, a tone or vibration is created that can be likened to radio waves sent by a transmitter. Many religions teach that these "prayer waves" resonate on the subtle realms of existence with angelic presences that assist us in our evolution. By praying for Divine grace and by surrendering to the rhythms of the Divine from a sense of emptiness and vulnerability, we open ourselves to the possibility of deep blessing. Prayer at this stage is a humble and loving act grounded in respect for our higher self and that of others.

Prayer from Stage Eight comes from our wholeness and our connection to our inner rhythms, as opposed to prayer from previous stages, which is often more procedural or wishful. In Stage Five (Merging), it was common for us to grunt, moan, yell or otherwise express the tones of the troubled areas of our being. In Stage Seven, we expressed the tone that builds the energy that discharges it. In Stage Eight, the tone expressed is one of unification among the aspects of ourselves that were once alienated from one another. As a result, the tone feels vibrant and alive.

In Stage Eight, we begin to use tone from voice and musical instruments to help us contact our bodymind's natural rhythms. Because tone is an organizing force in the universe, whatever prayer we choose in Stage Eight, we are using tone vibration to help unify our wholeness with the wholeness of spirit.

Repeating a certain holy word or sound, known as a mantra, can be especially powerful in Stage Eight. Although the mantra doesn't change the prayer itself, it changes our ability to experience the resonance of the prayer. To name just a few of these mantras: "Om," "Om Namah Shivaya," "Om Mani Padme Hum," "Nam Myoho Renge Kyo," "Hare Krishna, Hare Krishna, Krishna Krishna Hare Hare," "Sa Ta Na Ma," "Baroch Ha Shem" or "Inch'Allah." For some, the personal mantra imparted in Transcendental Meditation is effective, while others may recite the prayer of their religious teachings, like the Lord's Prayer or the Hail Mary.

Prayers of praise to the Universal Presence are an important aspect of many religions. Among Sufi mystics, whose spiritual traditions empty the mind of everything but tone and breath, the following prayer of praise is especially beautiful:

> The darkness of the night and the brightness of the day,
> the beams of the sun and the light of the moon, the

murmuring of the waters and the whispering of the leaves, the stars of the sky and the dust of the earth, the stones of the mountains, the sands of the desert and the waves of the oceans, the animals of water and land praise Thee.

Yoga. Yogic practices that involve disciplines like physical exercise, deep rhythmic breathing, meditation, and devotion can provide tremendous insight and integration in Stage Eight. In addition to yoga, other forms of gentle movement can be extremely helpful. Practicing T'ai chi, akido, the Five Rights of Rejuvenation, Continuum Movement, instinctual dance to quiet music, gentle swimming, and other forms of relaxed movement can promote integration because of our openness to experiencing the more subtle aspects of ourselves and the interconnectedness of our rhythms. At this stage of healing, these types of activities can effectively help us to connect with the next healing stage. Even observing a ballet, a Sufi dance, or other form of sacred dance or graceful movement can activate a feeling of wholeness.

Self-nurturing. I mentioned that Stage Eight provides a perfect opportunity to truly nurture ourselves. It is an ideal time to go on a meditative retreat or a transformational weekend so that the lessons learned in the previous stages can be more fully integrated into our total being. Experiencing a gentle massage, micromovement massage, Huna Kane temple massage, herbal beauty wrap, or relaxing in a hot tub, mud bath, mineral spring, or flotation tank are ways of honoring ourselves and often result in a spontaneous transcendental experience.

Being held by another person while we are in Stage Eight can be an especially enjoyable and integrating experience. A full body hug from someone supportive and loving — just for the sake of sharing the contact — can be profound. We actually "melt" into our partner. Synchronizing our breathing with that of another person during Stage Eight can also help connect us with our internal rhythms. In fact, this simple yet deep experience often moves us into the next stage of healing.

Seeking Help

In this stage of healing, working with a dialoging psychotherapist or engaging in art therapy, music therapy, energetic sound, or light therapy may help bring about further integration and wholeness.

As in earlier healing stages, I recommend chiropractic adjustments, Rebirthing, craniosacral work, and other healing systems that seek to empower the bodymind's natural rhythms, inner knowledge, and experience of wholeness.

Serendipity — the Natural Order

"Things happen" in Stage Eight. For example, let us say that you have been involved in a romantic relationship. Your partner went away for a while or was involved in a relationship with someone else. When you were without your partner and experienced the feeling of emptiness, you somehow knew from deep inside how important your relationship was and how things needed to be. In Stage Eight, it is from this emptiness that you may decide to enter a committed relationship.

As we begin to connect to our inner rhythms of wholeness, it is both easy and natural to perceive serendipity, which we were first aware of in Stage Six, as no longer strange or lucky. Instead, we know it is the natural way things work. We more clearly accept our rhythms and expect to be in alignment with the greater rhythms around us. We sense that our rhythm, the rhythm in our relationships, and the rhythm in the world around us are somehow all connected. It is not just a cognitive awareness, but a knowledge we can actually taste. It comes from deeply experiencing the connectedness of those rhythms with all our senses. But it happens only after the interference between ourselves and our natural rhythms has been reduced, which occurs between stages One and Seven.

Trusting the Change

Stage Eight is often the time when we choose to move to another city or country, change relationships, find a new job, or adopt a plant-based diet. We may also become concerned about the environment, or become more aware of the political or global consequences of our everyday actions involving diet, buying habits, or managing financial resources. Like the revelations we experienced in the earlier healing stages, these perceptions are not the result of trying to make them happen. They just feel correct. The choices we make in Stage Eight consistently work for us.

Friends who have not yet achieved Stage Eight will not be able to understand how we can change our lives and expect them to work without all the logical "necessary" preparation. They may play devil's advocate, attempting to let us know how frivolous or naive our choices are. They may think we've flipped our reality lid, and they are right! Our knowledge of the correct nature of what we "have to do" can truly be appreciated only by someone who has at least visited this healing stage.

The Stage Eight experience was reported in a recent *New York Times* article about Tibor Kalman, the innovative graphics designer, and his wife, Maira, the popular author of zany children's books. The article related the couple's "radical decision" to close their highly successful businesses, sell most of their belongings, leave their friends, and move with their children from New York to Rome. Maira Kalman's comments on the move are resonant with the Stage Eight consciousness: "We're reinventing our lives. You're suddenly vulnerable. Your senses are reawakened. It feels like falling into a vat of lemon mousse."

In Stage Eight, new and interesting people often come into our lives. This is the time when we meet people who uplift us and change our lives in positive ways. This is also a time when "magical" encounters and events occur that create new possibilities for us. These experiences may be new and bewildering at first. However, it is important to trust the processes and know that people who appear are there for a purpose. The idea of trusting ourselves was beautifully expressed in a letter by a doctor as she moved through Stage Eight:

> I have finally gotten a clue to what trusting oneself really means. For the first time in my life, my spirit and my educated mind went into battle and my spirit won. What a feeling of peace that brought! I also decided to go within, get my answers from within, and not be swayed by the externals. On a spiritual level, this has helped me so much and the support that follows is amazing to me.

In Stage Eight, gaining such insights becomes more possible as we continue to experience our internal rhythms. Again, the ability to sustain the connection with our internal and external rhythms is also a function of having learned the rhythms of the previous stages of healing. Now that we have healed enough to acknowledge the connections, we not only feel in alignment with the external rhythms of life, we also trust where these rhythms take us. During the later phases of Stage Eight, we trust that our experiences are mirrors and that everyone we meet is there to support our internal processes.

Making the Heart Connection

Finally, Stage Eight provides the opportunity for us to become integrated with our heart center, where we learn to truly love ourselves and those around us. This concept is beautifully expressed by David Roth in his song, "Will You Come Home?"

> Will you come home, will you come home.
> Will you come home to your heart?
> You've kept away from yourself from the start
> But you can come home now, come home to your
> heart . . .

Leave the baggage behind, you've done more than your
part
Before you fill all your loved ones, you must fill your
own heart.
Don't look to others for directions or deeds
You're the very first love that your heart ever needs.

After moving through Stage Seven, in which we left much of our old "baggage behind," we begin to hear our internal rhythms, often for the first time in our life. This inner listening brings with it self-acceptance, wisdom, and love. As a result, we come to the realization that each of us is truly the "first love" our heart ever needs.

If you have been in the presence of a spiritual master, a guru, or a holy person, you may have felt a connection with your heart center, an expansion of yourself, or a rhythm that gave you a sense of peace. You may have cried or you may have laughed when this meeting occurred. As you connect with your heart center, you will understand the feelings of emptiness that open the door to deeper levels of spiritual enlightenment. It is the emptiness Jesus spoke about that allows you to be filled with Divine Light. It is the emptiness the Buddha referred to that opens the door to enlightenment. Stage Eight is the portal to the higher stages of healing, which are connected to Divine Light, spiritual enlightenment, and the deep understanding of our connectedness to all life.

Hearing Yourself Ask for Help

Stage Eight is the first level of *being*. It is the doorway to the higher states of consciousness. Because healing involves gaining greater wholeness and responsibility, asking for help in Stage Eight is drastically different from the previous stages. You may say, "Thank you for guiding my steps, my thoughts, and my actions," or "Thank you for bringing me the people and events necessary for my unfolding." Note the gratitude expressed by the words *"Thank you."*

Instead of asking for a specific event, the prayer acknowledges the connection between outer circumstance and inner reality: "Lord, please continue to guide my steps. Please continue to bring people, events and situations to me that serve my highest good. Thank you."

Stage Eight Exercise

While sitting or lying comfortably, place the second, third, and fourth fingers of one hand on the lower portion of your breastbone. Then place the second, third, and fourth fingers of your other hand between your eyebrows. Bring both elbows far forward in front of you as comfortably as you can. Breathe in through your mouth, and slowly exhale through your nose. Continue for one to two minutes. Visualize your breath being directed outward simultaneously through the two points you are touching.

Stage Eight Declarations

"I wake up to my rhythms of wholeness."

"I take counsel within myself."

"I experience the fullness of my emptiness."

"I reunite with my whole self."

"I pay attention to myself."

"I trust my rhythms."

Stage Eight Exercise

9

STAGE NINE

Light Behind the Form

*I am the bulb and Thou art the light within it. The truth
and the miracle is this: Thou art the Bulb and the Light.*
— PARAMAHANSA YOGANANDA

Stage Nine begins what many people would call the transcendent
stages of the healing process. It is the second level of a state of
"be-ing," when we first experience a higher or altered state of consciousness. Although we are acutely aware of the physical forms
around us, we begin to perceive that life is more than the outward
physical manifestation: it is also the energy, the force, and the light
behind the form.

Life Force

Albert Szent-Gyorgi, the Nobel-prize-winning physiologist, said
that it takes energy to move the wheels of life. This universal energy, or life force, impregnates the entire universe and stands behind
all creation and evolution. The ancient Chinese called it *qi*. The Jewish esoteric teachings refer to the life force as *chai* in the book
Tanya. The word formed from these words, *Chaitanya*, means "life
force" in Sanskrit. The noted biochemist Rupert Sheldrake spoke
about the nature of this vital force in his book *The Rebirth of Nature:*

Energy is indeed present in all living things. Living

organisms draw it from their environment, as plants take it from the sun in photosynthesis and animals take chemical energy from their food through digestion and respiration. They accumulate it in their own bodies and use it to power their movements and behavior. When they die, the energy accumulated in their bodies is released to continue on its way in other forms. The flow of energy on which your body and your brain depend at this very moment is part of the cosmic flux, and the energy within you will flow on after you are dead and gone, taking endless new forms.

This vital force acts on the air we breathe and the food we eat. It creates and sustains living tissue. It is present throughout the natural world and may be why we feel revitalized after a dip in the ocean, a walk in the woods, or a picnic in an open field.

In the earlier stages of healing, we are largely unconscious of the presence of this vital force, and may actually deny its existence. However, in Stage Nine, we begin to experience life differently. As we arrive at this stage of healing, we become acutely aware that there is more to us than the physical body we have grown accustomed to knowing. We begin to perceive that there is a life force, an energy, an intelligence that flows through us. This energy can manifest as warmth, vitality, color, or light. It is not unlike the rush of energy we feel when we are in love with, or sexually attracted to, another person. Athletes often experience this feeling as a "rush" after an intense workout.

Like electricity, universal energy is neither good nor bad. It simply is. On an elemental level, it creates, maintains, and heals our bodies throughout our lives, and stands behind our ability to reproduce as a species. It also enables us to create beauty and harmony in the fields of art, music, science, religion, and politics. We affect everything around us according to how we express this energy.

The Stage Nine Experience

In Stage Nine, we begin to feel energy or life force extending through us and into the world around us. At the same time, we become aware that there is a deep yet subtle connection between ourselves and our environment, which includes the "empty" space around us, as well as other people, animals, and plants. We may not physically see this connection, but it is something we can experience with the heightened sensitivity that has unfolded. And this is only the beginning.

Simply acknowledging that we are more than our physical senses and that there is a force or an intelligence that flows through us can potentially change our lives forever. For perhaps the first time, we sense that we are part of a larger, *energetic* reality, as compared to merely a *physical* reality. And this broader perspective initiates our ability to view ourselves playing a small but significant role in planetary healing.

Again, Stage Nine can be experienced in a variety of ways, such as feelings of warmth, light, or vitality. It can also manifest in our bodymind as a tingling sensation, not unlike the feelings that Star Trek characters might experience just as the transporter beam is activated: as though their atoms are being taken apart and reassembled. Like them, the tingling sensation of energy we perceive in Stage Nine often accompanies the transition to a new reality of being. The following experiences reflect some of the ways in which it is perceived.

Monica was a practice member of a bioenergetic therapist. After moving through the first eight stages of healing, one day she experienced a powerful bioenergetic session. She later wrote,

> I walked into your office burdened with everyday problems. I walked out refreshed, content, composed, and ready to face my obstacles with a calmness and a sense of energy or life force I didn't have before.

Linda, a woman going to a breathwork practitioner, related the following experience after taking a weekend workshop:

> During a breath workshop, my legs, my hip, chest, arms and hands all felt numb. This even moved up into my face. I licked my lips, wondering if I could feel them. I couldn't move my hands. I was scared for a moment, and began thinking that I've got to get out of here. In a brief moment, my body went from being heavy and not responsive to what I wanted to do, to feeling very, very light. Energy started flowing through, in the same way that I felt the numbness creep in. It is as though I was electrified. Energy shot through my fingers and even my eyes. "This is definitely different!" I said to myself. For some strange reason, I laughed. It was probably the deepest belly laugh I had ever experienced. I felt happy.
>
> I now know that there is an energy, or some type of force, that flows through me. Even months after that experience I can "check out" or scan my body when I am upset, or when my breath isn't fully present. It is very important to me now because I actually am in touch with the "companion" of the energy or force going through me. When it is not present I realize that I am out of touch with something that I need to connect with once again.

Peter received a deep tissue massage at a health spa. While he was on the table he felt the spasm in his shoulder and the pain between his shoulders release. At the same time, a prickly feeling radiated from his shoulder blade into his shoulder and into his arm. Seconds after this sensation began, Peter experienced what he described as a warm flow, as if heated oil was making its way through a blocked channel. His hands and feet became warm. He began to experience a smile that lasted for days.

A practice member named Lisa wrote to me relating her ongoing Stage Nine experience after a chiropractic adjustment:

> During a session, you evoke a response from my nervous system that clears out the physical end emotional blockages in my spine. On an experiential level, I feel my life force flowing through my body as this happens. This contact with a positive force is always present, and is not under the control of my conscious, usually analytical mind. It is a humbling and spiritual experience. . . . The wonderful thing is that I haven't had to use my conscious mind to elicit this response. *The experience of feeling unlocks the effect.* And it continues, even between sessions.

For some, the experience of this energy or vital force manifesting in the bodymind may feel like a wave or pulsation moving through them. Some people's bodies actually move in a wave-like undulation as blockages to this flow are released. I call this a soma-to-psychic wave because the energy in this wave exchanges information dynamically between the body (soma) and the mind (psyche). This experience often occurs with certain forms of yoga, bodywork, Network Chiropractic, Somato-Respiratory Integration, or some breath-oriented therapies, in which an individual has an emotional release, feels empty afterward, and then immediately expresses an involuntary wave-like pulsation in parts of the body or in the entire body.

Experiencing this energy provides us with the knowledge that it is real, powerful, pure, true, connected beyond the physical form, and somehow related to joy, beauty, excitement, and vitality. After the emptiness in Stage Eight, perceiving the life force naturally brings deep feelings of gratitude, as if our plates were empty and are now being filled with delicious food. Stage Eight sets the stage for the joy

and gratitude which is necessary to experience the life force in Stage
Nine. In fact, the phenomenon of perceiving these waves of energy
does not make it a Stage Nine experience unless it is accompanied
by feelings of peace, simplicity, joy, or happiness. Childlike feelings
of naivete and awe, as well as a rush of excitement, are also characteristic of the rhythm of Stage Nine.

Heightened Perception of Light

As we move from the emptiness associated with Stage Eight, we
begin to experience a greater perception of Light, within ourselves
and sometimes in others. This light not only reflects our vital energy, but is the Light of wisdom, compassion, healing, and understanding. Rarely is this perceived as something new. When we begin
to see it, we realize that it has been there all along, but somehow we
were blocked from its radiance. *The Celestine Prophecy* by James
Redfield contains nine prophetic insights. Insight Number Three
states,

> We humans will learn to perceive what was formerly
> invisible types of energy. . . . The basic stuff of the uni-
> verse, at its core, is looking like a kind of pure energy
> that is malleable to human intention and expectation in
> a way that defies our old mechanistic model of the uni-
> verse.

Because thought or expectation causes our energy to flow into
the world and affect other energy systems, Redfield goes on to say,

> Human perception of this energy first begins with a
> heightened sensitivity to beauty. . . . The perception of
> beauty is a kind of barometer telling each of us how
> close we are to actually perceiving this energy.

I mentioned that when we reach Stage Nine the bodymind is

often very sensitive. Not only do we see physical forms more acutely, but we also begin to perceive the energy with our inner sight. This faculty is called *clairvoyance*, which literally means "clear seeing." As a result, Light can sometimes be seen as an aura or energy field radiating from all living beings. The experience of seeing energy fields has been discussed in literature and poetry. It is most often associated with a spiritual insight or the experience of love.

When I was in undergraduate school, I took several classes in art history. I noticed that many religious paintings by European masters of the fourteenth, fifteenth, and sixteenth centuries depicted energy fields around religious figures like Jesus Christ, the Virgin Mary, the saints, and most angels. Early paintings from the East — including those of India, China, Japan, and Tibet — showed the same type of energy field around pictures of the historical Buddha, the Lord Krishna, and other Hindu gods and goddesses. Biblical stories spoke about the spikes or horns of light coming from Moses's head as he descended Mount Sinai with the Ten Commandments.

In addition to the human aura, energy centers in the body, called chakras, have been depicted in the East for centuries. Each chakra is a swirling center of energy exchange and has a specific role to play in our lives. Both ancient and modern proponents of these Eastern traditions teach that we possess seven major chakras, which correspond with the seven glands or organs that are part of this system of exchange.

In modern times, the human energy field has been measured by special film that is highly sensitive to electromagnetic radiation. This process is called Kirlian photography. Radiations from the body have also been recorded as temperature by using thermography, which involves scanning infrared heat emissions from the body and producing a special color photograph of those findings. Some chiropractors use thermography to help correlate nerve transmission levels in different parts of the spine. Other instruments have been developed that can measure the body's microwave radiations for diagnostic or analytic purposes. The use of nuclear magnetic resonance imaging (MRI) as a replacement for X-ray is based on the concept that each tissue of the body emits its own specific magnetic field. The patient is placed in a highly induced magnetic field, and a computer monitors the changes in their tissues as they are detected by a magnetic device. The computer then generates a picture based upon the interaction of the patient's magnetic field with that of the diagnostic tool.

In Stage Nine — as in other healing stages — the experience of perceiving energy fields is not something we need to figure out. We simply know that the energy is there, that it is flowing through us, and that it is somehow connected to us. And once we become aware of, or connect to, any aspect of our being that we had not fully experienced before, we begin sensing it more freely in ourselves and can start perceiving it in others as well.

Working with the Energy

There are many kinds of energetic or magnetic healing disciplines available. *Qigong* is an ancient Eastern tradition of using the life force for healing. Other Eastern disciplines, like T'ai Chi, Tae Kwon Do, and other kinds of martial arts and yoga, teach us how to work with this healing energy.

The concepts expressed in Stage Nine are inherent in the development and evolution of the chiropractic profession. Daniel David Palmer, the discoverer of chiropractic, sought to create a healing system that would unite humanity's physical and spiritual natures. His intent was to create a union between the structural and the energetic approach to healing that would encompass the whole person.

The expression of an inherent life force is also consistent with the development of healing systems like acupuncture, shiatsu, and homeopathy. Other modalities, such as Somato-Respiratory Integration, Therapeutic Touch, Reiki, Rebirthing, Huna Kane, breathwork, and Hands of Light, are also based on working with life force for healing.

The pioneering psychiatrist Wilhelm Reich spoke of the life force as *orgone*. To the degree that humans are able to experience this orgone energy flowing through them, Reich believed that they were more able to express their full physical, psychological, and spiritual potential. Alexander Lowen and John Pierrakos further refined this concept in creating bioenergetics, and Core Energetics respectively. As health practitioners become more familiar with the concept of energy, its use in physical, emotional, and spiritual healing will become a more accepted aspect of their practices.

Huna Kane, the ancient Hawaiian temple initiation, is a form of massage that uses this vital force. Burt, a fiber optics engineer working with the National Aeronautics and Space Administration, wrote about his experience with Huna Kane bodywork, which affected both himself and Sandra, the bodyworker:

> After a few minutes, I decided to start playing with the energies present. I felt the energy flow through me and radiate outward. I started sending back to Sandra some of the consciousness and love she had imparted. I felt more and more energy flowing down my upstretched arm, and my other arm pointing towards her. . . . Our energy fields met and meshed. The transfer started, meridians activated, *qi* energies pulsated — the energy fields grew and focused. The cosmic dance engaged. A peace and calmness remained. I was aware and quite whole, integrated and alive.

Please be aware of Burt's reference to love, awareness, peace, and calm. Again, this is an important part of the phenomenon that makes this a Stage Nine experience. In Stage Nine, we don't always need a teacher to show us how to use or direct the life force energy, although one may be appreciated. In Burt's example, his experience of the energy taught him how to use it.

In the Tantric tradition, this force is called *kundalini* "the serpent power." Tantra yoga uses special breathing exercises and other methods to raise this energy through the spine. As it travels through the spine it energizes the chakras until it finally opens and awakens all the spiritual centers.

When people are stimulated artificially through hallucinogenic drugs or the unguided practice of certain kinds of kundalini yoga, they can be awakened prematurely by the kundalini force. This often brings more energy than they can handle and can result in physical or emotional problems that are sometimes difficult to correct. However, if they have fully experienced the previous eight stages of healing, this "awakening" is as natural as any other body process.

Gratitude and acknowledgment of the flow — as opposed to manipulation of the flow — are characteristics of Stage Nine. When we are in Stage Nine, we do not think of what we are trying to do with the energy. Instead, we observe it with a sense of awe and wonder without trying to change it. In Stage Nine there is no ego investment. There is no desire to balance or redirect, but simply to experience, observe, and share.

As with all stages, we do not need to change anything. We merely need to be in harmony with the stage we are in, whether for ourselves or for others. This involves acknowledging what is present in the moment. Respecting and honoring what is observed is enough for it to be transformed on its own accord.

Activating Stage Nine

As in Stage Eight, prayer, chanting, and reciting mantras can be effective in activating the Stage Nine experience. Meditation; deep breathing techniques; hatha, kundalini, mantra, and tantra yoga (when practiced under the guidance of a qualified yoga instructor); whole brain-type work; and ingesting certain psychoactive plants as a sacrament have been used to more fully experience this healing stage. Vigorous exercise that releases endorphins in the brain and enables us to achieve an athlete's or runner's "high" can also open us to feeling the life force characteristic of Stage Nine.

Fully resonating with the rhythms of Stage Nine may be

considered a mystical experience. By surrendering to its rhythms, you may find, for example, that your breath will deepen and your head will roll backward. Your breath will expand in your upper chest and will move through your shoulders and even into your lower neck. Your breath will feel as though it is coming in through the bottom of your spine, spiraling up your spine, traveling through and out the top of your head.

If you are lying on a massage or chiropractic table, your arms may naturally drop to your sides or stretch above your head. Your legs may separate, as if you are straddling a table. You may sit up spontaneously and start rocking at the base of your spine. Your breath may feel like a cloud, suspended inside and outside your body. You may feel the energy within as the sensation of life force.

A metamorphosis is occurring. Your thoughts begin to break up. They are no longer patterns of thinking, but are perceived as thought forms or energy packets. When a thought enters your consciousness, you see it slowly unravel into energy. If you mentally drop a pebble anywhere into your being, you experience the solid form dissolving and feel the ripples of energy it makes throughout your entire bodymind.

Moving Through Stage Nine

At times, people who are in Stage Nine may move to earlier stages to better learn their lessons and develop a stronger sense of integration. When they return to Stage Three, for example, they feel stuck, but instead of feeling stuck because of physical pain, a reoccurring emotional problem, or a relationship difficulty, they may be aware they are stuck because their energy is not flowing freely. Again, just because we are aware of our energy flow (or lack of flow), or we can perceive the energy in others, does not mean we are in Stage Nine. This stage must be accompanied by the joy, gratitude, and love that naturally accompany states of consciousness that allow us to accommodate a greater expression of our spirituality and thus our wholeness.

At this stage of healing, we realize we are not who we thought we were. We discover there is more to us than we have ever experienced. We become aware of our direct energetic connections to our environment, and realize that we are responsible for this vital force and how we express it in the world. We are aware that we can always draw more on this energy as a resource for continued healing, wholeness, and understanding. We realize that the reality we experienced before was extremely limited. Now, if we do not experience the energy, it feels as if we are missing something.

This awareness occurs as Stage Nine is completed. In the early part of this stage, we are excited and startled as we begin to feel the energy field and may actually begin to "play" with it. In the middle of Stage Nine, we are in awe of the process we are experiencing. As the stage concludes, we understand the rhythm that tells us that, "There is an energy that flows through me, there is a consciousness that I am made of, there is an aspect of my reality I have never known before. I am not a fixed product or body, but I am in the process of unfolding." This understanding opens us to new paradigms in life as we experience being in awe of this vital life force. As the stage concludes, we wouldn't consider playing with this energy, but simply seek to honor it.

Seeking Help

In most cases, stages Nine to Twelve require a healing facilitator instead of a curing-type practitioner. The experience of life force is outside the "norm" of the medical model, and by focusing on symptom care the curing practitioner may not be able to assist you at this stage.

If you feel you need a psychotherapist or emotional counselor while in Stage Nine, find a practitioner who uses energy work as the foundation of his or her practice, such as a Reichian, Jungian, bioenergetic, or Core Energetic therapist; a psychosynthesis practitioner; or someone trained in Holotrophic breathwork. Healing facilitators who don't have the concept of a vital energy or life force at the core of their disciplines not only can distract the individual in Stage Nine from healing, but also can induce fear or lack of trust in the healing process.

A Note of Caution

If Stage Nine is not the natural result of moving through the previous stages, there is a danger of having the energetic experience without the joy, the love, the rhythm, and the strengthening of one's sense of self as it begins to dissolve into a new reality. Simply put, we must be "someone" before we can be "no one." Before we can modify our sense of self — through experiencing a new "energetic body" and the vital force characteristic in Stage Nine — we must be secure in who we are.

Some people have a sudden experience of energy flow, such as that produced by psychoactive drugs, a meditative experience, or a kundalini event induced by a method of breathing or yoga postures. This energetic awakening may be associated with fear or pain if it occurs without the consciousness or rhythm of Stage Nine. If they have not been grounded in a secure sense of self, the experience can involve further physical, emotional, or psychological trauma, causing them to move to the lower stages of healing, especially stages One and Two. But by moving through the stages once again, they can later reclaim the Stage Nine experience with all its magnitude.

It is also common for individuals who have a history of marked trauma — such as physical, emotional, or sexual abuse — to feel uncomfortable when they experience energy moving through them. Unless the nervous system is free of interference and mechanical tensions, the experience of the spiritual flow, or the awareness of the flow of life force, can often activate responses characteristic of stages One and Two. If this occurs, use the exercises presented for the stage you have returned to. Practicing those exercises can help you more fully integrate the experience and assist you in moving toward Stage Nine from a place of groundedness and alignment.

Hearing Yourself Ask for Help

Gratitude and awe go hand in hand with Stage Nine. Therefore, when asking for help you may say something like, "Thank you for this life force and may it continue to flow through me" or "Please help me experience my energetic connection within myself and others."

Stage Nine Exercise

There are two exercises which express the Stage Nine consciousness. Perform the one that feels most appropriate to you. The first is to lie comfortably on your back, with your legs apart and relaxed. If you are lying on a massage or chiropractic table, let your legs straddle the table. Imagine a cloud of light above you. Open your arms — as you would if you were holding a large beach ball — or stretch them above your head. Breathe the cloud of light gently yet deeply in through your mouth and breathe it out through your nose. Do this for at least one or two minutes.

Another Stage Nine exercise is to lie on your back in the same fashion, but instead position your arms as if you are going to do a headstand. Bend your elbows and place the palms of your hands flat on the table or floor at shoulder level or behind your neck. Breathe in through your mouth and breathe out through your nose until the rhythm takes over and your breath and movement become automatic. Otherwise continue for at least one or two minutes.

Stage Nine Declarations

Stage Nine calls for acknowledging the Universal Intelligence, or the life force, passing through us. In other words, we acknowledge the light behind the form.

"I experience my vital force."

"I experience my inborn intelligence."

"I experience my energetic connection with the world."

"I am grateful."

Stage Nine Exercises

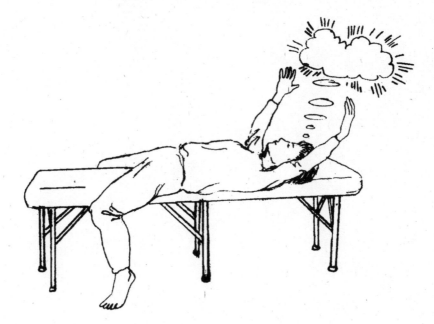

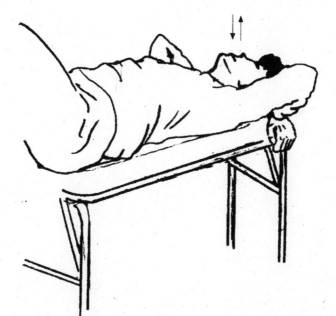

10

STAGE TEN

Ascent

Be still and know that I am God . . .

In Stage Nine, we experienced the life energy and felt ourselves filled with light, intelligence, and love. The Stage Ten experience dissolves our sense of self as separate from the rest of the world.

The tenth stage of healing is the ascent stage. Although not the highest stage of healing, it is the most sought after. Ascent is the stage that mystics, gurus, and other religious leaders from both Eastern and Western traditions have long spoken about. This state of consciousness has aspects similar to *nirvikalpa samadhi* in Hinduism, *knana samadhi nvdanta* in Zen, and the stage of effortless insight culminating in nirvana in Buddhism. Sri Aurobindo called it "the overmind," and among Kabbalists, this state is parallel to *chesed-chomach*. Christian mystics call it the "Christ Consciousness," and transpersonal psychologists sometimes refer to it as "transpersonal integration."

Aminah Raheem described this stage of healing in her book *Soul Return:*

A sense of separateness — from oneself, others and the

environment — is replaced by an inner attunement to a great natural Order. Surrender to that Order . . . becomes possible and appealing. A sense of well-being and integrity will automatically accompany these knowings.

For those of us seeking spiritual enlightenment, healing, or a sense of connectedness with all of creation, the consciousness and rhythms of Stage Ten are usually the highest expressions of what we are seeking. For those of us who have moved through the previous nine stages of healing, Stage Ten is the "reward" for our efforts. It is the stage when we relinquish our sense of self completely and merge with Universal Consciousness. As a result, we open ourselves to new realms of existence. Bernadette Roberts described this feeling in *The Path to No-Self*:

> Let us say that one day we went to the window and discovered that we could no longer even feel it, no longer feel the sense of self as a separate existence — what could be said of this? Evidently, someone has removed the window and, when we went to feel it, we simply fell out, literally fell out of our self.

Our sense of self can be viewed as a candle. Up to this point in the healing process, we may have a very bright candle, shining with the light of our being. As we move through Stage Nine, we become aware that there is a bright light outside and it is coming into the room. Suddenly we realize that our candle does not appear as bright as it was before. And if we walk outside into the brilliance of the noon sun, it appears that our candle is no longer lit. This is the concept of how our sense of self is relinquished in the vast brightness of the Universal Consciousness of Stage Ten. It is not unlike the experience of the Apollo astronauts when they landed on the moon. When they looked back at the Earth they were forever changed, because their smallness in relationship to this magnificent planet became apparent to them.

Being the Light

In Stage Nine, we experienced being filled with energy or consciousness. In Stage Ten, rather than intelligence or consciousness expressing itself through us, we *become* the energy, we *become* the consciousness. As opposed to feeling the love within us, we *become* the love.

In Stage Five, we merged with the nonintegrated rhythms within ourselves. By contrast, in Stage Ten, we merge with the unrecognized *wholeness* of our being, which we call "alienated wholeness" or "nonaccessible wholeness." In this stage we feel safe, connected, embraced, and embracing. We are both observing and being observed; it is an experience of both seeing ourselves and experiencing ourselves beyond sight.

In this stage of healing, we transcend time, as if it no longer exists. We also transcend space, as if we are no longer aware of where we are. In Stage Ten, there are no more polarities and dualities: it is no longer us and the universe because we feel that we *are* the universe. We feel our connectedness to the wind, the light, the rain, and the earth. We also feel deeply connected to every living thing. By the time we reach the Ascent stage, our consciousness has expanded to such a degree that it encompasses everything. There is no separation between ourselves and everything around us.

This unitive and loving consciousness was spoken about in Carlos Castaneda's *Tales of Power*, when Don Juan described another shaman named Genaro:

> He was just now embracing this enormous earth but since he's so little all he can do is swim in it. But the earth knows that Genaro loves it and bestows on him its care. That's why Genaro's life is filled to the brim and

his state, wherever he'll be, will be plentiful. Genaro roams on the paths of his love, and, wherever he is, he is complete.

The Eightfold Experience

Paramahansa Yogananda, the renowned teacher of Kriya Yoga and founder of The Self-Realization Fellowship, taught that the Divine flow of energy and connection with the Supreme can be experienced in eight ways: light, sound, peace, calmness, love, joy, wisdom, and power. For many, the interpenetration of these terms make up the Stage Ten process, because we rarely experience each attribute separately. There is no distinction between "up," "down," "inside," or "outside" in Stage Ten because there is no longer any separation between ourselves and the world around us.

In Stage Ten, there is no light versus darkness, because there is only light. We feel our whole being is light and tone, as if we have lost all our density. We feel so light, and so "of light," that we may expect to open our wings and fly. Often we may assume yoga postures spontaneously, or our bodies may experience ecstatic waves moving through them. It is like an orgasmic-type rush that goes beyond sexual feeling. Like the molecules of water that merge with the wind to give substance to waves, our waves of feeling represent our ecstatic merger with the Absolute or the Supreme.

A practice member reported Stage Ten as being a great wave that encompassed his total being:

> What else is there to accept but the flow of life? At times it's hard to see that it's just a wave, but when you are experiencing it, that's all it is! You get caught up in the wave, and you don't know which way is up or which way is down. But you don't care. Sometimes you ride on top of the wave and you feel that somehow there is a way that everything can get worked out, even though you don't yet know what needs to be worked out.

Sometimes you become part of that wave. It stares you right in the eyes and you know at that precise moment that you are free. You are safe and you are joyful. There is no fear, no regret, doubt, or unfulfilled expectations. There is no judgment or feeling the need that "I've got to do something." All is light, all is perfect. The "now" moment is a sublime place where one can seek the presence of the Higher Power caressing one's heart, as one's heart is connected to the Higher Power. It is an experience of security, and comfort and release.

Everything we contact in Stage Ten enriches us. When we experience love, we experience wholeness. When we become love, we become whole. When this transformation occurs, there is no longer a need to be loved or to be whole again. Our entire reality shifts because we are awake, just like Sleeping Beauty opening her eyes after a deep sleep.

In Ascent, images, visions, memories, and insights may pass before us. Tones may be heard; sensations may be felt. It doesn't really matter what the content of the awareness is at the time: what matters is the *person* who is observing, feeling, and healing. The individual who experiences is the only reality.

If we are truly in Stage Ten, we are not thinking about our experiences; there is no ego and no sense of ourselves as personalities. For this reason we are unable to make comparisons or judgments, nor are we proud of our achievements. Our essential experience is rediscovering our oneness and connectedness with all we experience.

After a spinal adjustment during a Network Chiropractic seminar, a healing facilitator reported what could be described as a Stage Ten experience:

During the adjustment I was spirit connected to all. And I felt fire from my insides as if they were yelling "I'm alive, I'm alive." This new rebirth in me was an ecstatic experience. As "I'm alive" rang through my body, I became somehow connected to both more of me and less of me, yet without terror, without denial, without anger, without feeling rejected. I felt that being alive was a glorious opportunity. . . .

A practice member once exclaimed, "My life was orderly and predictable most of the time. Then healing came along and everything got turned upside down." In Stage Ten the conscious mind has lost its reference points. The information exchange between the newly discovered field of consciousness and ourselves is immense, because our sense of self has dissolved itself in this unity state. The intense love that is available for our expression in Stage Ten can now merge with our educated minds or our unconscious reality. As a result, the experience of Stage Ten establishes a new level, foundation, or base in our evolution as human beings. For many Stage Ten is a time of absolute chaos. But it is chaos guided and cushioned in Divine essence.

Gurumayi Chidvilasananda said, "God does not mean someone living in heaven. God is the light which exists in every person's heart." When we experience this awareness without needing a mediator, such as a rabbi, priest, minister, guru or therapist, we are spiritually awake. These individuals may assist us in our connection, but they are no longer the connection itself. We are grateful for their help, but our *attachment* to their role as an intermediate has shifted profoundly. We see, we taste, and we experience something that transforms us. There is no greater fulfillment. There is no greater contentment. There is no greater excitement, insight, or relaxation. It feels as though we have come home. The more we express this state, the more at home we feel.

But Stage Ten is not always a blissful experience. (In fact, we can still have disease symptoms and experience Stage Ten.) At times this mystical stage provides powerful insights into our existence that reach the very depths of our soul. The following letter from a practice member reflects this facet of the mystery of Ascent. Carolyn had two miscarriages before she began Network Chiropractic care. Although neither child was born alive, the type of language she uses and the description of the experience is characteristic of a Stage Ten experience.

> The first son died in 1984, in the womb two weeks past the due date, and the second died in 1987, six months after conception.

> After both [still]births, we held the babies and spent time with them. From the moment of my first Network Chiropractic experience one morning, my entire being focused on these children. There was no precise thought or emotion, but just a profound awareness of them in every molecule of my being. This continued throughout the morning, and after lunch I went to a Rebirthing class. I cannot begin to convey all that I experienced, but suddenly at some point I was both infused with and surrounded by a beautiful radiating rainbow of light. Out of that beautiful light emerged a vision of my two sons as I had seen them and held them after their birth, yet in my vision they were fully alive, radiating light and love. They free-floated and smiled at me, radiating the purest joy that I have ever felt.

> When I regained my normal consciousness and stood up, I was overcome by the greatest sadness that I have ever experienced. The Rebirthers lovingly hugged me, sat me down, and wrapped me in blankets. I tried to understand where this sadness was coming from after what I thought was one of the most joyful of events.

Later that afternoon, I returned for another chiropractic adjustment. While I was on the adjusting table, I heard Charley Thweatt's song "Be Still and Know that I am God" on the sound system. Suddenly, I was at a point where I felt that I was pure energy connected with everything and everyone. I became aware of the children once more, except that my awareness wasn't visual. I knew with all certainty that what I was experiencing were the spirits of my sons. With this connection, the bonds that never happened, happened. And they set us all free. That experience was both the happiest and saddest moment of my life.

No Expectations

Throughout this book I have stressed the importance of surrendering to the stage of healing you are in as opposed to striving to reach a higher stage. This advice is especially important regarding Stage Ten, because this is the stage most people want to experience and remain in forever.

I have found that people who seek enlightenment often take longer to attain and integrate the Ascent stage of healing into their life than people who have no expectations of eventual enlightenment. In some cases, the conscious desire to surrender their sense of self and obtain peak religious experiences may actually distract them from the healing process.

For some reason, those who are consciously seeking transformative spiritual experiences often have much work to do in the earlier stages before transformation is possible. As a result, they often return again and again to the earlier stages after briefly glimpsing Stage Ten. By contrast, those who fully experience their sense of self in the earlier stages, without considering the idea of peak or mystical experiences, often find it very easy to achieve that experience. It almost always comes as a surprise. At the same time, the integration that occurs during the earlier stages provides the bodymind with the capacity to more deeply experience Ascent, as opposed to perceiving only a small glimpse of it.

This does not mean we should abandon our religious teachers, discard our holy books, and give up our spiritual practices, yoga exercises, meditation, or prayer. When used to help us resonate with each stage of healing — rather than to provide an escape from our reality — such assistance can be very helpful to further the healing process. But when used as an escape or as a denial of what is, this assistance can actually be a distraction that can delay or prevent achieving union with the Divine and the healing it brings.

In the twelve stages of healing, *surrendering ourselves fully to the stage we are in* empowers us to move to whatever stage is necessary for our healing at exactly the right time. A chiropractor wrote,

> Ascent found me when I was least looking for it. It found me and took me on its wings. I began to feel a strong sensation throughout my body. Waves and vibrations washed through me. As I looked around the room, I knew with every cell of my being that I was connected to everyone, physically, emotionally, mentally and spiritually. Common boundaries of space and time ceased to exist. A glistening white light surrounded my vision. When my eyes were closed, the light was opalescent and beautiful beyond description. For three hours, the light and waves were so strong that I could not — and did not — want to walk. The waves continued to a lesser degree for over three weeks, reminding me of the vast beauty of the Universe. The exquisite beauty of this epiphany experience will be with me always.

Many people in our Western society have read about mystical or spiritual experiences involving union with the Supreme or oneness with God, but cannot relate to them. Others have euphoric or peak experiences and don't know what to do with them because they have not yet created the foundations necessary to properly integrate these experiences into their lives. As a result, the experiences exist only as memories.

When a true Stage Ten experience occurs, it is more than a peak experience. It changes our lives. The experience of a Universal Intelligence or God occurs when the nervous system is open and flexible enough to merge with it. Rather than being the result of personal expansion, the spiritual experience naturally occurs when Divine energy touches the cells of our body, completely changing the reality of our cells and bringing about transformation.

Flowing Through Stage Ten

In the Ascent stage of healing there are many methods that can enhance our experience, yet they are best discovered instinctively. The methods, techniques or practices we choose will naturally lead to a life of acceptance — as opposed to rejection — of our humanity and the natural world around us. Some of the most enlightened modern mystics and humanitarians — including Thomas Merton, Mahatma Gandhi, Albert Schweitzer, and Peace Pilgrim — always went to nature for inspiration and enlightenment. This is one reason why those who perform yogic practices often experience Ascent. Yoga (a Sanskrit word meaning, literally, "to yoke or to harness") embraces both the physical and energetic aspects of our being.

Scientists are beginning to consider nature as a basis for the discovery of the infinite. The Nobel laureate and pioneer in brain research Dr. Roger Sperry said,

> What happens is that biologists have been searching the wrong places. You don't look for vital force amongst atoms and molecules — you look instead among living things. Among living cells and organisms acting and interacting as entities. In other words, the special vital force that distinguishes living things from nonliving are

emergent, holistic properties of the living entities themselves. They are not properties of the physio-chemical
components, nor can they be fully explained in terms of
physics and chemistry. This does not mean that they are
in any way supernatural or mystical. Those who can see
vital forces in supernatural terms are just as wrong as
those who deny their existence.

In *The Reach of the Mind,* Norman Cousins commented on poet
Walt Whitman's view of the mystical as part and parcel of the natural world.

> Whitman sensed that the activities of all life forms —
> from the quail whistling in the woods to the shark's fin
> cutting through dark water — are related to each other
> in a manner more sophisticated, and indeed more "intel-
> ligent," than we are usually inclined to believe. Vital
> forces, not reducible to mere material fact, work
> throughout the universe to constitute what Whitman
> called "the exquisite scheme" of creation. What we often
> dismiss as mere "nature" or "the natural" is in fact a sub-
> tle, complex web of life that is no less mysterious sim-
> ply because it surrounds us everywhere. On the con-
> trary, what is most natural — what is everywhere and
> touches life daily — fascinates us and frightens us the
> most. . . . Whitman postulated a type of intelligent net-
> work, a mutually recognized, natural vital force that
> binds all forms of life together in the evolving universe.

Clear Channels with the Divine

In Stage Ten, we become connected to the field of Universal
Consciousness, and we are open to the knowledge, wisdom, and

inspiration this field contains. In this stage, we are able to receive information, which may be artistic, scientific, religious, or philosophical, that appears to come from a place outside the normal thinking self. Sometimes this process is considered channeling, in which people in a light trance are inspired by another presence and may speak or write words that move spontaneously through them. In Stage Ten, we are no longer our normal thinking self because we have expanded to a point in which "self" now includes other realms of possibility.

In Stage Ten, people often receive wisdom from the spirit realms and attribute names to its source, such as God, Buddha, Allah, or Christ. Others refer to spirit guides or discarnate philosophers, musicians, or scientists. Receiving wisdom directly from the spirit realms is nothing new. The biblical tradition in Judaism, Christianity, and Islam teaches that the Prophets heard the word of God and shared it with the world in the form of oracles. The Prophets were seen as individuals who connected to higher realms of Divine Consciousness in which God or angelic beings could speak directly to them. A *maggid* or spiritual teacher was believed to have spoken to Joseph, informing him of the purity of his wife, Mary. The Prophet Jeremiah said he felt God touch his mouth and use phrases such as "It is I, Yahweh, who speaks" and "The mouth of the Lord has spoken."

In Matthew 10:19–20, Jesus tells his disciples not to worry about what to say when they are arrested: "But when they deliver you up, take no thought of what ye shall speak: for it shall be given you in that same hour what ye shall speak. For it is not ye that speak, but the Spirit of your Father which speaketh in you."

The experience of the Muslim prophet Mohammed is best known among members of the Muslim faith. It is believed that a transcript of a tablet from heaven was revealed to him by the Angel Gabriel, which was the word of Allah, or God. The information this heavenly tablet contained became known as the Koran, the holiest book in Islam.

The Vedas are ancient Hindu scriptures that are the most sacred of the Sanskrit works. Written in the form of poetic hymns, the Vedas were believed to have been given by gods and goddesses in the heavenly realms to highly evolved seers and spiritual adepts on the shores of a sacred Himalayan lake. The root word for Veda is *vid,* meaning "Divine knowledge." Later, Hinduism and the practice of yoga began placing greater emphasis on the importance of personal experience rather than on Divine revelation. Guru yoga developed, in which the practitioner would experience the inner guru as teacher.

Tibetan Buddhist teachings also speak of wisdom passed directly to humans from deities and other discarnate beings. Their best-known teachings are found in *The Tibetan Book of the Dead.* The name "Kaballah," the book of esoteric Judaism, is derived from the term *QBLH,* which means "to receive." Other traditions speak of guardian angels who provide individuals with guidance and assistance, and people throughout history were believed to communicate with them.

Plato reported that Socrates had an inner voice, whom he called Damion. It acted as a protector and warned him of danger. Joseph Caro [1488–1575] was a rabbi who received his guidance from a being called The Soul of Mishnah. Joan of Arc was said to have begun hearing voices at the age of thirteen. She reportedly saw visionary figures she said were Saint Michael, Saint Margaret, and Saint Catherine. She called them her "council." Joseph Smith, Jr., the founder of The Church of Jesus Christ of Latter-Day Saints (Mormons), was said to have translated scriptures from records inscribed on golden plates shown to him by an angel named Moroni.

Since the Middle Ages, organized Judeo-Christian religions have assumed that the days of prophesy are over. Although the books of each major religion were obtained by prophetic insight, the religions they inspired consider insight by prophesy or channeling invalid and even demonic. For this reason, mainstream Western religions no longer have a functional role for prophets. Ministers, priests, rabbis, no longer officially function as channels of Divine Wisdom. As a result, there are no sanctioned contributions to contemporary Jewish or Christian doctrines through channeling. With the exception of "fringe" religious groups and new-age channelers, prophesy and revelation have almost ceased.

Therefore, it is no surprise that our society does not have a place for people who function in Stage Ten and receive information from the Universal Consciousness. There is even less opportunity for them to share the knowledge gained from the Stage Ten experience.

Expressing the Wisdom of Stage Ten

When we move into Stage Ten, the lesson we learn from its rhythm is of our connection to all existence. This experience changes us and often provides deep insight and wisdom. After this connection is made, what we do with the insight is of great importance.

Although we can communicate in Stage Ten, it is not through words, because words and thoughts are no longer adequate in this realm. In Stage Ten our internal communication is through light, tone, breath, and movement. People in this state of consciousness seem to communicate with non-verbal cues such as hand gestures, glances, touch, or movement. Others in this stage somehow know without a doubt what they are experiencing, without a word exchanged.

Words generally relate to things in one of three tenses: past, present, and future. In Stage Ten, however, consciousness is timeless and does not fall within our usual realm of time-bound thought. We are in an altered state of consciousness relative to our thinking state. There is no separation between us and the field of consciousness we are in. To communicate with words we must have polarity; when there is no "me" or "you," verbal communication is not possible. Even our internal dialogue is based upon a sense of separation between the "speaker" and "listener." (If there was no separation, we wouldn't need to communicate anything.) For this reason, information received in Stage Ten must be communicated through the consciousness of another stage.

Ideally, if we have fully incorporated the healing of the earlier stages into our being, we will move on and communicate our Stage Ten consciousness in stages Eleven and Twelve. But if the pure consciousness of the Ascent stage activates any dissonance in our bodymind, the information we receive in Stage Ten will often be expressed through the consciousness of the earlier healing stages.

For example, if the wisdom gained in Stage Ten expresses itself through the consciousness of Stage Two, our interpretation may be to criticize and judge others, especially those who do not know or accept our newly gained insights. If the insight is interpreted through Stage Three, we will perceive others as being stuck and resistant.

The religious concept of false prophets may refer to people who have received information from God, but are expressing this wisdom through one of the earlier stages of healing, as opposed to the later stages of Eleven or Twelve. As a result, it is often distorted and destructive information. Rather than being healing, unifying or uplifting, such information often leads to divisiveness, suffering, and condemnation of others.

The expression of Stage Ten's pure consciousness can only be understood and communicated when our consciousness is clear enough, integrated enough, and expanded enough to perceive the totality of the Stage Ten message. For this reason, communicating the infinite reality of Stage Ten to others is often fragmented and partial. By being aware of this possibility, we spare ourselves (and others) a great deal of difficulty.

With each stage of healing, we gain access to a larger "keyhole" through which we broaden our perspective of the world. In Stage Ten, we experience a quantum leap in expanding our view of reality, of ourselves, and of the universe. The challenge is to take the Stage Ten perspective and view it through an even larger keyhole, thus providing a greater vision. This is what happens when we move into Stage Eleven.

Hearing Yourself Ask for Help

In Stage Ten, you are no longer separated from the Source from which you ask for help. Specific thoughts and words have minimal meaning in Stage Ten.

Stage Ten Exercise

Lie on your back with your legs bent, feet on the floor. As you breathe in through your mouth, gently raise your hips off the floor and tilt your head back gently until your chin is pointing up. While you do this, raise your arms and join your hands in front of your forehead in a classic gesture of prayer. Drink in air with your mouth, making the sound of the wind as you breathe.

As you breathe out through your mouth, lower your hips and lower your hands, yet maintain their praying position. Your fingers will now be pointing between your legs. As you connect with the rhythm of this stage (which is likely to be within one minute when you are truly in Stage Ten), your body may tend to arch in response to your union. Repeat as often as you wish. Rest for at least 15 minutes after this exercise. Your reality will be truly altered and a few moments time to integrate your experience is necessary before going back to your routine.

Stage Ten Declaration

Since words are not easy at this stage, resonating with the concept of "I am One" spontaneously occurs as you embrace Stage Ten.

Stage Ten Exercises

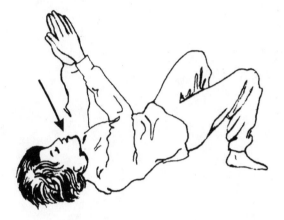

11

STAGE ELEVEN

Descent

It is right in the midst of life that we have to develop and express all that is beautiful and perfect and divine in our souls. — PIR-O-MURSHID HAZRAT INAYAT KHAN

After experiencing the grace of Stage Ten, we know that the source of power, love, and consciousness is universal. It does not come from us; it does not come from others; it does not depend on the outer events or circumstances in our lives. Instead of a conceptual understanding of our oneness with this Divine Source, we know it to be true at a cellular level. We incorporate this understanding into the deepest aspects of our being.

Stage Eleven resonates with the conclusion of the story of the Greek hero Odysseus. Over a ten-year period, Odysseus endured fierce battles, dangerous storms, the encounter with the Cyclops, a battle with the cannibal Laestrygons (in which he lost most of his men), and an adventure with the nymph Circe, who could turn men into swine. Odysseus wins Circe over, and becomes her lover. She then takes him to the realms of the underworld where he meets the blind sage Tiresios, who teaches him male and female knowledge. After Circe directs him to the Island of Light, Odysseus experiences the light and is then tossed back into the sea, whose currents take him home. He reunites with his wife, Penelope, and returns to earthly existence with the wisdom gained from his incredible adventure.

The previous stages of healing are not unlike Odysseus' journey. In our healing journey, we also experienced suffering, fear, and courage. We fought monsters, merged with our illusions, and discharged what we no longer needed. We learned the mysteries of our being and merged with the Universal Light.

An interesting aspect of our healing journey is that it involves moving from stage to stage rather than remaining in one stage. This was also true for Odysseus, as related by Joseph Campbell: "A significant feature of this great epic of the inward night-sea adventure is its representation of the voyager as never wishing to remain at any of its stations."

Like the varied experiences in Odysseus' voyage, each of the twelve stages is a temporary place of learning on the healing journey toward home or wholeness. And like Odysseus' visit to the Island of Light, we cannot remain in Stage Ten forever. Ascent involves being in a state of Universal Consciousness, healing, and love. But human evolution offers us the opportunity to express this healing, love, and consciousness where we live, which is on the earthly plane. In the words of the renowned meditation teacher, Jack Kornfield, "You have to live your spirituality day to day, at home, at work, in your car. Otherwise, it won't transform you, and in the end you won't benefit and transform the world around you."

The Stage Eleven Experience

If we have fully experienced the rhythms of Stage Ten (Ascent), our lives are no longer what they used to be. Although we are still involved in human relationships, earning a living, cooking meals, and taking out the garbage, in Stage Eleven we now descend into our lives with new perspectives, more energy, and greater understanding. As a consequence, we no longer feel isolated from the Source that we experienced in Stage Ten. We become like the tree that is rooted steadfastly into the ground, whose branches reach into the sky. We begin to live from the experience of being one with the Source of unlimited consciousness and we act accordingly in daily life.

In Stage Eleven, our relationships change. We no longer compete with others for their energy or attention by being possessive or jealous. And we no longer need to give others our energy because it is no longer an issue of "ours" or "theirs." We now feel ourselves to be a channel of universal energy; we know that it simply exists.

We are like flowers that offer their perfume and beauty. They don't care if they are appreciated; they don't offer more of their beauty to some people and less to others. Their task is to live in the world and offer their beauty and perfume without reservation. One of the challenges of Stage Eleven is to live in the world and offer others our best, according to our unique talents and abilities. We are "giving our gift," and do so from a place of groundedness and insight, without feeling special or self-important. We simply are who we are.

In the Descent stage of healing, our intuition brings us more into alignment with life's natural rhythms. We perceive ourselves as being conduits of the universal coherent rhythms in all we see, hear, breathe, and touch. We uplift the situations around us because we no longer become hooked into the drama of, or attachment to, our experiences.

A basic lesson of this stage is to sustain gratitude and remain in awe of the miracle of life while we perform our daily activities. To the degree we are able to function from our true self and our natural internal rhythms (as opposed to reacting to the alienated, dissonant aspects of our nature, as in the earlier healing stages), we can serve as powerful agents for service and healing in the world. This affects us individually, and it can have a profound impact on our relationships with others and the greater community. In *A Treatise on White Magic*, Alice Baily wrote,

> When man functions as a soul, he heals; he stimulates
> and vitalizes; he transmits the spiritual forces of the

universe. . . . Humanity's function is to transmit and handle force. This is done in the early and ignorant stages destructively and with harmful results. Later, when acting under the influence of the soul, force is rightly and wisely handled.

In Stage Eleven, we realize that we are responsible for the expression of the energy we receive and how it affects our lives and the environment. In his book *Shambhala: The Sacred Path of the Warrior*, the Tibetan teacher Chogyam Trungpa eloquently discusses the responsible use of this energy for healing and unification:

But you can invoke and provoke the uplifted energy of basic goodness in your life. You begin to see how you can create basic goodness for yourself and others on the spot, fully and ideally, not only on a philosophical level, but on a concrete physical level.

New Perspectives

Being aware of our distortions and transforming them in our lives is part of this healing stage. Nick Gordon, president of Emissary Foundation, related a story about how this change of consciousness occurred in his life when friends gave him a surprise birthday party. In the midst of the celebrations, a beautiful cake was brought out, which Nick recognized as cheesecake. After blowing out the candles and with the hostess looking on, Nick took his first mouthful and began to gag. It was the worst-tasting cheesecake he had ever eaten! Desperately trying not to offend his hostess, he was about to ask for a napkin so he could spit out the cheesecake, when she said, "This is a new recipe. I made a banana cream pie and put the bananas through the food processor. I hope you like it."

Nick suddenly realized that he had been stuck in a perspective: he was eating banana cream pie, which he thought was cheesecake! He realized that because of his assumption and judgment he was unable to accept the gift that was being offered. With his rapid change in perspective, he began to savor the taste of the pie which he found to be absolutely delicious.

In Stage Eleven, we attract people, events, and circumstances that offer opportunities to liberate ourselves from old perspectives and help us further our growth and evolution. As in Stage Eight, but even more so, we are aware that life is attracting them to us.

As we move into Descent, we also become aware that our thoughts are essentially distractions from focusing on our inner reality. We become aware of how we have distracted ourselves throughout our life by our concepts, comparisons, analyses and attachment to habits. The Dalai Lama discussed the importance of focusing on our inner reality:

> Liberation cannot be sought from the outside through something else, like someone else giving it to you. When one has achieved liberation by means of removing all afflicted emotions, then no matter what kind of external conditions one meets with, one will not generate any of their afflicted emotions. Thus one will not newly accumulate any new karma. The cycle has been stopped.

> Therefore the attainment or non-attainment of liberation depends upon the removal or non-removal of the afflicted emotions, the chief of which is ignorance. The process of liberation depends on the removal of the afflicted emotions, and that depends on wisdom. Wisdom, in turn, depends upon the intention to definitely get out of cyclic existence. Initially, it is very important developing the intention to leave cyclic existence.

Thinking: From Distorted to Magical

Rather than adhering to the past and the future, in Stage Eleven a new kind of thinking occurs that creates new realities for us. This kind of thinking is called "magical thinking" by the noted physician and holistic healer, Deepak Chopra, M.D.

> By magical thinking I mean the expecting of outcomes just by the mere desire to have them. We are all familiar with people who have a desire. When it spontaneously manifests in their life without any effort on their part, that's magical thinking. I have a desire for strawberry ice cream. You walk by me and say, "Hey, Deepak, would you like some strawberry ice cream?"

To our amazement, we saw in Stage Eight that flashes of this magical thinking sometimes occur. However, in Stage Eleven, our entire lives become strongly guided by this thinking.

After the unitive experience of the Ascent stage, we realize that we are recycled earth, water, and air. The same web of intelligence that creates the stars and the rain forests creates us as well. By striving to remind ourselves of this truth, we begin to participate in magical — or reality — thinking once more. Rather than just being aware that magical thinking occurs (as in Stage Eight), we now find that it actually becomes the foundation of our thought. There is simply no other way of thinking for us.

One challenge of Stage Eleven involves avoiding involvement with trivia: the background noise in our consciousness, the old ways of thinking, the projections of contemporary society, and the adherence to old images and situations that had caused us distress in the past. In Stage Eleven, we are more conscious than ever before that by indulging in old perspectives, we lose our connection with the network of intelligence that connects us with everything.

As we descend into the "lower" realities of daily life, we are able to clean up remaining interference. This stems from our direct experience and active participation with Universal Consciousness while in the Ascent Stage. We do this with the awareness of our inner potential and our commitment to this consciousness. Because we have already gotten in touch with that part of our self that is beyond words, time, space, our body, and emotional images, we know it is there for us always. We realize we can exist on the earthly plane while knowing that true existence is not of this world. It is of a time-less, spaceless, all-knowing and all-loving intelligence that tran-scends the time/space of daily existence.

In Stage Eleven, we realize that healing (as well as life itself) occurs only in the present. We exist both in the now moment and in the eternal, which are in essence the same. Dr. Chopra spoke of this timeless awareness and its role in healing. When asked "How do we heal?" he responded:

> Through transcendence. There is no other way out. To see things with the crystal clarity of pure awareness not through the old memories, not becoming a victim of the stale repetition of old memories. So we reexperience pain, sorrow, anger, guilt, physical conditions with this new awareness, no longer being attached to them, observing them, observing ourselves, observing the action.

His idea resonates strongly with the Stage Eleven consciousness, because it opens us to view events and challenges from the per-spective of the larger picture. It also illustrates how the way we think can affect our health. For example, imagine that you are about to go bungee jumping. If you are terrified by the prospect of jumping off a bridge with an elastic cord tied around your ankles, your brain will produce a neurochemical called norepinephrine, which can con-tribute to the risk of hypertension, atherosclerosis, and heart attack. Fear and related feelings of hopelessness are linked to the produc-tion of other neurochemicals that can decrease immune response, promote aging, and diminish sexual desire.

By contrast, you can get ready to jump, look down at the same deep chasm, marvel at the view, and be excited about the prospect of flight. You do not feel that you are being violated by the forces of the jump because you are whole and are not judging the forces of gravity or the recoil as good or bad. As a result, your brain responds by producing neurochemicals like endorphins, which increase your overall sense of well-being. Other neurotransmitters strengthen your immune system, protect you from cancer and other viruses, and increase your sexual desire.

In the earlier healing stages, our responses were often controlled by the alienated and fragmented aspects of our being. However, the healing that took place by moving through the first ten stages has enabled us, in Descent, to respond to life's challenges from a state of wholeness, strength, compassion, and integration. In this stage we have the cognitive choice to meet life from either perspective, because life more immediately and clearly mirrors our inner reality.

If someone doesn't love us, in Stage Eleven we are no longer hurt by it because we know we *are* love. There is no longer a dependence on others to bring us praise, validation, or attention. Of course, it still feels good when someone expresses their love to us. However, our day is generally not ruined if this does not happen. If we radiate love without conditions — which is how it was given to us by the universe in Stage Ten — we learn more and more that love is not to be received from others. Instead, love is something to be experienced and shared.

Expressing Stage Eleven

Throughout history, enlightened spiritual masters, philosophers, scientists, inventors, composers, poets, writers, and artists were able to gain insights and inspiration from Stage Ten and communicate them through the nonattached yet loving state of Stage Eleven. Many of their ideas were not well received when they were offered to the world. The teachings of Jesus were viewed as radical and dangerous during his lifetime, resulting in his crucifixion as a revolutionary. Some of Mozart's compositions were considered obscene by concert-goers, who subjected him to anger and ridicule. The paintings of Courbet, Monet, Van Gogh, and Kandinsky shocked the Parisian art world.

When we are in Stage Eleven, our ideas are sometimes not well received because they come from a perspective that is different from those shared by contemporary society. However, it really doesn't matter to us if our ideas are not well received, because magical thinking has created and brought them into existence. Authors, artists, musicians, philosophers, and healers do not create paradigm shifts. Their books, paintings, musical compositions, scientific research, and healing methods do not revolutionize thought. Instead, they serve to transmit the consciousness of the Universal Paradigm Shift that has already occurred and to which these individuals were attentive and responsive. In other words, they do not change the world; they merely respond to the paradigm shifts that have already occurred. To lead the way requires individuals who are in Stage Eleven.

The Crucible of Earthly Existence

For many who move into Stage Eleven, the circumstances we experience in daily life (such as discord with our partner, a pain in the arm, or an asthmatic condition) still remain. As we move through these life situations with greater awareness, we often revisit one or more of the earlier stages of healing, and continue to heal those aspects of our being that are interfering with the expression of stages Nine, Ten, and Eleven.

Returning to the earlier stages offers us opportunities to reevaluate many of our beliefs, relationships, lifestyle habits, and aspects of our lives we once thought were important. Alan Cohen addressed the importance of reevaluation and reflection from this perspective:

> If money could make us happy, millionaires would rest complete. If sex could fulfill us, those who enter relationships or marriages based upon sex would roam no farther. If power were the source of peace, heads of

state would be the happiest people in the world. But persons with money, sex or power are not always the happiest; in fact, they are often the most unhappy. Why? Because only those who are constantly *discovering* are fulfilled. And discovering is not something that happens to us . . . it is something we *do*.

Revisiting the earlier healing stages is an integral part of the process of reevaluation and discovery. Although it is not always pleasant, daily adventures and challenges create the perfect context for us to grow, to heal, and to assist others in their healing processes. More than sixty years ago, the Sufi teacher Pir-o-Murshid-Hazrat Inayat Khan addressed the importance of being in the world:

> Man need not go into the forest away from all people to sow his goodness and virtue. Of what use is his goodness and virtue if he buries himself in the forest? It is right in the midst of life that we have to develop and express all that is beautiful and perfect and Divine in our souls.

Living Stage Eleven

Stage Eleven is both exciting and precarious. We take risks to express what we have already learned in our healing process, often to people who have not yet experienced the later stages of healing. Because we have already experienced the early stages (often many times over) we understand how others feel because we have been there, too. This creates a sense of humility as well as compassion.

We realize on a cellular level that life contains the spirit of our union with God. Enthusiasm (from the Greek *entheos*, meaning "embodiment of God") becomes an integral aspect of our daily lives. Part of the enthusiasm and strength we experience in Stage Eleven is due to the momentum toward wholeness that our healing has created for us.

New perspectives have been established. New insights have been integrated into our being. Therefore, as we move through Stage Eleven — which involves descending into our daily lives again — an important shift in consciousness takes place. We may encounter the same kinds of circumstance we encountered before, but our intimate awareness of the field of consciousness, our experience of love (and our being an expression of that love), change the way we experience the world. In Stage Eleven we can participate in daily life, yet no longer react to it in the same old way.

A good example of this shift in consciousness took place in my office a few years ago. Helen had been in Stage Ten. She was lying on the adjusting table, giggling and smiling, with a euphoric look on her face. Her body was arched, and she was breathing as if she was drinking air. After a while she left the table, nodded at me, and smiled. The only communication she wanted to express was through hugs and smiles.

Helen then left the office and went to her car. She discovered that someone had hit her car in the parking lot and the front end was completely destroyed. Although she did not have much money and the car had been very important to her, when she saw that the car was smashed, her only response was to laugh. She later exclaimed, "Thank God I wasn't in it!" It was not just a thought she had, but her entire physiology responded in gratitude because the car had been smashed when she was not in it. She then added, "It's only a car. It doesn't know how to heal. . . . I do." Helen's jovial reaction to what is often seen as an unpleasant event is characteristic of Stage Eleven consciousness.

In Descent, we may ask ourselves, "How do I feel about how I feel?" Even if we feel miserable, we can still feel joy within the misery. Yet this would be incomprehensible for someone who has not experienced this stage of healing. In Descent, we have merged with the essence of Universal Love and the consciousness we experienced in Stage Ten. When this merging is the spontaneous result of moving through the previous stages of healing, a natural state of grace is always carried with us.

During a particularly challenging period of my life, I was distressed that I had not taken the time for prayer. When discussing this with my wife, Jackie, she responded with Stage Eleven wisdom, "Don, you don't have to be distressed by not taking time to pray. You can make every breath, every movement, every action you take a prayer. The way you greet people and touch people can be your prayer. The kiss you give me can be your prayer. Do you really need to separate this time as work time, that time as play time, and other time as prayer time? Can't they all be interconnected and simultaneous? Why not make your life a prayer?"

A Blessing

In Stage Eleven, you wish to give your blessing to everything and everyone. But first you give this blessing to yourself. You recognize that a prayer is a blessing. You recognize that whatever you focus your magical thinking upon you intensify. And when you place your attention on anything, you help pray for it from whatever rhythm you are presently in and bring more of that rhythm into your world. Therefore "negative thinking" is a prayer or blessing in reverse. In Stage Eleven, your awareness of the oneness of creation blesses everything you consider.

Toward Stage Twelve

In Stage Eleven, we experience magical thinking and observe ourselves perceiving the world around us. We feel full of light and what may be considered by others as goodness. At the same time, we realize that this goodness does not come from us and does not belong to us. We begin to see ourselves as mere channels or temporary vessels for light, love, and wisdom.

As we complete this healing stage, we become increasingly aware of the quality of our interactions as we further connect to the external rhythms around us. And as we fill ourselves with goodness — while living in the world — we master the lessons of this stage of healing.

The Sufi master Nawad Jan-Sishan Khan said, "A candle is not here to illuminate itself." Now we come to realize that we need to move to the next stage of our healing journey, which involves becoming aware that the light we are filled with is not meant for us alone. By its very nature it is to be shared with the greater community. In *Shambhala: The Sacred Path of the Warrior* we read,

> What the warrior renounces is anything in his experience that is a barrier between himself and others. In other words, renunciation is making oneself available, more gentle, and more open to others.

This consciousness represents the transitional point between Stage Eleven and Stage Twelve.

Hearing Yourself Ask for Help

In Descent, you may say, "Dear Lord, please guide my movement through life in love and in light, without attachment to my circumstances," or "Dear Lord, please make my words and actions in this world a representation of thy Will."

Stage Eleven Exercise

Stand with your feet apart, shoulder width. Bend your knees slightly and rock your pelvis back and forth (barely noticeable).

With your right hand, fold your little and ring fingers against your palm while joining your thumb, index, and middle fingers. This is the traditional hand gesture used in blessing. Hold your left palm open, yet relaxed.

Maintain these hand and finger positions and gently bring your hands to your chest, right hand over left, as if you are cupping your heart. As you do this, bend your neck forward and slightly bend your knees. Breathe in through your nose. Exhale through your nose as you open both hands and slightly rotate them inward, as if you were about to clap your hands. Maintain the same right hand and finger position. As you exhale, tilt your neck backward and slightly arch your back. Do this rapidly about ten times, then let yourself slow to a natural pace.

Repeat, allowing the rhythm to connect with you. Hold the position as long as it feels natural.

Stage Eleven Declaration

"I express my divine gifts."

"I illuminate all my circumstances."

"May it be on Earth as it is in Heaven."

Stage Eleven Exercise

12

STAGE TWELVE

Community

The modern quest for community is a quest for one's person-
hood. . . . The essence of community is wholeness . . . that meets
my needs and those of the greater whole of which I am a part.
Community is a deeper reality within which I move and have
my being. It is one of the names of God. Community is a gift of
myself, what I give in endless participation with my world.

— DAVID SPANGLER

By the end of Stage Ten (Ascent), we experience communion with the Universal Intelligence, Universal Love, and Universal Consciousness that interpenetrates all creation. In Ascent, there is no longer a marked sense of self, because it has been obliterated by the enormity of the Universal Consciousness we are experiencing. The consciousness of Stage Ten activates a new awareness of the gifts we have to offer the world: our individuality, talents, life experiences, compassion, and wisdom. Although these gifts may have always been with us, we can now express them without the interferences characteristic of the previous healing stages, such as fear, alienation, guilt, or old perspectives.

In Stage Eleven (Descent), our "I am" consciousness is reestablished as a new and expanded sense of self, and we move into our relationships with others no longer tainted by, or attached, to our past. We experience magical thinking and observe ourselves observing the world. We are filled with light, enthusiasm, and what others consider to be goodness. We know that the life force is not ours, but belongs to the Source of Universal Love and Universal Consciousness; we are temporary channels for this energy so that it can manifest in the world for the greater good of all. We learn that we do not just commune with ourselves or our circumstances, but with the larger rhythms that are greater than ourselves and connect to everyone and everything around us. After leaving Stage Eleven, we take this consciousness into Stage Twelve, the stage of healing known as Community.

In Stage Twelve, we realize we are no longer passive observers. We find that healing is associated with our active participation in life. This includes our internal community, comprising the myriad aspects of the bodymind, as well as our ongoing communion with our wounds, joys, and sorrows.

The Meaning of Community

The term "community" comes from the Latin *communis,* meaning "common." The words communication, communal, communion, and community imply sharing, finding common ground, and experiencing relationship with ourselves and others. The state of community exists first in consciousness; it need not apply to a physical location, but is rather a way of being.

Our primary community is that of our bodymind. We are made up of quadrillions of cells, with each cell having a unique task to accomplish and a special role to fulfill. Cells are organized into tissues; tissues are organized into organs and organ systems. When this vast internal community works in harmony, we grow, heal, and fulfill our tasks in life.

Community may also include our primary relationship with another person. Marriage is perhaps the most respected form of community, because it serves as a foundation for society. In a primary relationship, not only do we experience community with our mate, but with our partner's relatives and friends as well.

We may have a community based on shared interests with others, such as our house of worship, school, food co-op, environmental organization, condominium complex, women's or men's center, or professional society. Community can also manifest as an intentional spiritual community, such as Findhorn, Abode of the Message, Sunrise Ranch, or Mount Madonna Center.

The concept of community plays an important role in many myths, legends and fairy tales. Community often represents the happy conclusion of the story, when the hero or heroine returns to a "home base" of friendship, protection, and harmony.

For example, "Beauty and the Beast" ends with a strong reference to community:

> "Now," said the Fairy to Beauty, "I suppose you would like me to send for all your brothers and sisters to dance at your wedding?" And so she did. And the marriage was celebrated the very next day with the utmost splendor, and Beauty and the Prince lived happily ever after.

In this case, community involved all her brothers and sisters at the wedding, with dancing and singing in ritual celebration.

At the conclusion of "Cinderella," we learn about forgiveness and merging in the creation of community:

> The two sisters recognized her for the beautiful person whom they had seen at the ball, and threw themselves at her feet, begging her pardon for all the ill-treatment she had suffered at their hands. Cinderella raised them, and declaring as she embraced them that she had pardoned them with all her heart, bade them to love her well in future.

> She was taken to the palace of the young prince in all her new array. He found her more beautiful than ever, and was married to her a few days afterward. Cinderella was as good as she was beautiful. She set aside apartments in the palace for her two sisters and married them the very same day to two gentlemen of high rank about the Court.

Cinderella and her sisters resolved the shadow or dark side of their relationship, merged with it, and transformed its energy to establish community. In this story, community was created among unlikely individuals with sharply divergent energies. Cinderella brought the divergent energies of her sisters into her heart through forgiveness, gave them apartments in the palace, and found them life partners of their own so they could, like herself, live happily ever after.

The tale "Ali Baba and the Forty Thieves" from the *Arabian Nights* addresses the permanence of community over the generations:

> "Open sesame!" He went in, and . . . brought away as much gold as he could carry and returned to town. He told his son the secret of the cave, which his son handed down in his turn, so the children and grandchildren of Ali Baba were rich to the end of their lives.

This story not only speaks about the community of Ali Baba's family, but the importance of passing on the secret of the cave for the benefit of future generations. This may allude to the secret oral teachings in some religious traditions that were handed down from the elders to the younger members of the community.

Participation With the Natural World

As we have seen throughout this book, a primary cause of suffering, disease and disharmony comes from our not being in touch with our wholeness. The impediments to wholeness are a result of not moving through the stages of healing and not feeling whole enough to experience the Divine energy within us.

What is understood and experienced as we journey through our healing process is that we are always connected to the Source. In reality, it is only our inability to perceive this connection that creates our suffering to begin with. It is the illusion that we are separate and disconnected from all that we are really connected to, especially our union with the creative force of the universe.

The idea that the universe is one great organism, with each part serving its separate function for the whole, is shared by many native and traditional societies, including Native Americans. After the Middle Ages, however, the mechanistic view of life — the universe as one big machine — gained popularity and laid the foundation for much of contemporary science, economics, and politics. Vice-President Al Gore addressed this issue and how it has led to our present social reality:

> And just as the false assumption that we are not connected to the earth has led to the ecological crisis, so the equally false assumption that we are not connected to each other has led to our social crisis.

The mechanistic model separates us from Universal Intelligence — the source of all creation — and diminishes the importance of our active participation in the world. By contrast, the vitalistic principle promotes the view that the universe is one body and that all life is interconnected. It teaches that the whole is greater than the sum of its parts.

It is impossible to create a well-working community that is based on incorrect, inadequate, or incomplete beliefs. Any concepts of science, economics, sociology, religion, or healing that do not create joy, compassion, humility, love, and a sense of personal responsibility for our choices are not truly valid. Any social system that separates people from each other is not resonating with the later stages of healing and must go through a transformation toward wholeness. Now is such a time for this to happen.

Writing in *ReVISION* magazine, Dr. Willis Harman, president of the Institute for Noetic Sciences, spoke of our ancestral tradition of communion and participation with the natural world:

> For a person living in the medieval world (as in many traditional societies), life is a seamless whole. Rocks, trees, rivers and clouds are wondrous and alive; the world is enchanted, infused with spirit. Human beings feel at home in nature; the cosmos is a place of *belonging*. . . . The universe is alive and imbued with purpose; all creatures are part of a Great Chain of Being, with man between the angels and lower animals. The working of enchantments, the occurrence of miracles, the presence of . . . beings with supernatural powers are — if not commonplace — assumed to be quite real and consequential.

Sadly, much of modern humanity has lost this enchantment. Many people have lost their connection to Earth and have ceased to consciously participate in the world. As a result, social, economic, and political decisions are based upon disconnectedness and alienation from the world community. This fosters lack of responsibility for our involvement with the world or with others. War is waged against our fellow humans, animals on the farm, and animals in the forests. It is easy, then, to destroy trees, deface the land, pollute water and air, and further develop technology that reinforces the same pattern. This disconnection has led to treating the Earth and her children as little more than commodities to be bought, sold, and used as desired.

These things do not happen because society is evil. They happen because of ignorance of our true nature and our inability to feel truly alive and magical. People who are disconnected from their source of love do not perceive themselves as dishonoring others because their actions are reflections of their own dishonor. This does not make them right, and it does not make them wrong. It simply reflects where they are in their understanding.

Acts of dishonor and abuse occur because we do not feel our connection to the world around us, which is impossible to feel unless we feel our connection within us. The more we honor ourselves and our internal rhythms, the more this honor will extend to the larger rhythms of the world. If we are in alignment with our natural flow, we may feel that spilling a barrel of chemical waste into a lake is almost like pouring it on our living room floor.

In Community, we find the places within ourselves where we have lost our participation. To the degree that we do not participate with ourselves as a community, we are unable to participate in the world around us. We need to awaken from our sleep so our reality can once again be transformed through our participation in the world.

The Participatory Scientist

In Stage Twelve, we become participatory scientists in every aspect of our lives. We become more aware of the illusions, fabrications, and distortions that keep us from being in touch with the larger reality around us. Our use of language, for example, often separates us from active participation in the world. Insurance companies sell us health and life insurance as opposed to sickness or death insurance. When we bring animals to a veterinarian to have them destroyed, we say we are "putting them to sleep." Rather than eating bull, cow, or pig, we eat hamburger, pork, sausage, or bacon. We don't send criminals to prison, but to a correctional facility.

As we continue to heal, we notice that community has always been present; it is only our degree of participation in the community that has varied. And only by our involvement in the laboratory of our individual healing can we truly experience our inherent community. When we observe the cooperative relationship among all the body parts, we recognize that the body itself is an amazingly exquisite community. And we see that illness occurs whenever a dysfunctional state exists within our community.

Dr. Harman wrote, "Wholeness implies that all parts belong

together and partake of each other. Each is a part of the whole; each participates in the whole. This *participation* is an implicit aspect of wholeness." He also stressed that "A willingness to be transformed is an essential characteristic of the participatory scientist."

The twelve stages of healing could also be called the "twelve stages of wholeness." If we imagine our wholeness extending in a circular fashion, each time we go through the twelve stages, our circle widens. In the early stages, the circle sometimes becomes narrower so we are able to focus on areas of our bodymind that need our full attention. As we heal those aspects, the circle begins to widen again, and it provides us with greater perspective and depth. This natural movement of expansion and contraction within the twelve stages is consonant with the cyclic rhythms of the universe.

Sharing our Wounds

In Stage Twelve, we come to true community when we have healed enough to share our gifts, including the wisdom and understanding gained through our healing journey. It is also a stage in which we continue the process of learning and discovering through interaction with others.

Nick Gordon, whom I quoted earlier, said, "In community I find the wounds I brought. This is one of the purposes of community." The wounds that Nick speaks about are those that may have inspired us to begin our healing journey, much like the heroes and heroines of the fairy tales, myths and legends we discussed.

According to Jean Houston, writing in *TANTRA: The Magazine*, wounds can be considered sacred because they contain the seeds of healing and transformation.

> The wounding becomes *sacred* when we are willing to release our old stories and to become the vehicles through which the new story may emerge into time. When we fail to do this, we tend to repeat the same old story over and over again. If you have a neurosis or

psychosis, it probably originated in pathos that was not worked out to its source in a Larger Story. If we would only look far enough and deep enough, we would find that our woundings have archetypal power. In uncovering their mythic base, we are challenged to a deeper life.

Healing is an ongoing process that continues throughout our life. In the healing system presented throughout this book, we move back through the early stages of healing to continue to heal alienated aspects of our being. Through sharing our gifts, which include our wounds, we continue the ongoing cycle of healing.

Like Descent, at first glance Stage Twelve can appear to be a letdown, because part of us yearns for the harmony, grace, and spiritual ecstacy we experienced in Ascent. We may think, "After all this work, I wish this could last forever." But Stage Ten is a stage we visit. We cannot live there. As human beings, our task is to live on Earth, our home for evolution, learning, and service. However, as we saw in Stage Eleven, we can now draw on the energy, the insights, and the love we experienced in the Ascent stage and manifest them in our daily lives.

Leadership and Consensus

When we speak of our inner community, we know that innate wisdom, through the nervous system, coordinates the bodymind, including every living cell. At the same time, these cells express consensus by sending messages back through the nervous system, which is received by innate wisdom. When each cell feels purposeful, respected, and integrated into the community, a healthy bodymind is the result.

This kind of leadership and consensus is especially evident in the lives of athletes. As peak performers, they are striving for community within their bodies, for leadership and consensus so that all their body parts will work together. In this community, the intent of each part is to express its self-identity and serve its function through its unique gifts for the benefit of the whole community called the body-mind. To the degree athletes have moved through the twelve stages, their community of cells, organs, nerves, and tissues will work together in harmony. Each part will communicate without the armor, protection, or learned interference characteristic of the early stages of healing.

At the same time, aspects of their bodies that are ignored, abused, or alienated and have not moved into Stage Twelve will seek their attention. This dissonance enables athletes to continue their healing processes. As a result, they gain an increasingly greater sense of community in their bodymind as whole, integrated, dynamic individuals.

Like athletes, we cannot successfully participate in Stage Twelve unless we have developed our sense of self and experienced the uniqueness of who we are. In Stage Ten, our identity or sense of self was dissolved and merged with Universal Consciousness. In Stage Eleven, that identity was established once more, but in respect to serving the larger picture. In Stage Twelve, we are now compelled to share our gifts with others.

An Expanded Perspective

When the members of the Apollo space mission landed on the moon and took the first photographs of Earth, a major shift in the concept of world community took place. To the astronauts, Earth appeared as a living organism of tremendous beauty and vulnerability, floating alone in the emptiness of space. This realization was a humbling, yet profound spiritual experience the astronauts shared with the rest of humanity through photographs and interviews. Col. Edgar Mitchell was one of those astronauts. As a result of his experience, Mitchell formed the Institute of Noetic Sciences to help bring spirituality and healing into a global perspective.

It is human nature to draw boundaries or imaginary "circles" around our lives. Some people draw these circles around themselves and their experiences to the exclusion of everyone else. Others expand their circles to include family and friends. Many enlarge their circles to include members of their religious denominations or those who share their nationality, race, or political beliefs. As we move through the twelve stages, our perspectives broaden and our circles of community expand to include more people, more beliefs, and even other forms of life. Like the healing process, expanding our perspectives is an ongoing, never-ending process.

Divergent Energies

In Stage Twelve, as we expand our circles to include broader perspectives, we often draw divergent energies (like arguments, disagreements, and conflict) to us. However, as we increase our sense of community and connection to others, we find that arguments, disagreements, and conflicts are only labels we place on divergent energies as a means of drawing attention to them. And we find that what appears to be chaotic on an obvious or immediate level is the basis of order within a larger context. For example, what appears to be an argument between two people on one level is really the result of their forming too small a circle because of their limited perspectives.

Rachel and Kenneth had many heated discussions over the purchase of a new car. Rachel wanted to buy a small car because it uses less fuel and causes less damage to the environment. Kenneth felt that a larger car is safer and more comfortable. Although they appeared to be at a standstill, Rachel and Kenneth reflected on their differences and searched for ways to resolve their problem.

One day Rachel discovered that some large cars that use natural gas (like the ones used by utilities and government agencies) were available to the public. They deliver good fuel economy and reduce the emission of harmful pollutants. For Rachel and Kenneth, their early arguments served an important purpose: to help them clarify their needs and concerns. By expanding their perspectives regarding alternative fuels, they found a solution that was acceptable to both.

In a true community, whether it be a physical community or a state of consciousness, situations naturally occur that challenge us. In Stage Twelve, we identify the situation as being related to divergent energy, and rather than ignore it, compete with it, or repress it, as we may have done in the past, we can ask ourselves these questions:

1. What is the opportunity that has been created?
2. How can I maximize this opportunity?
3. Who in the community can offer their gift to resolve the situation so that all of us are involved and all of us are enriched?

In our model of community or Stage Twelve consciousness, we discover that divergence is necessary for us to grow sufficiently so that we recognize that all people have gifts to offer, regardless of how obscured they may be. When we as individuals are healed sufficiently, we can receive them (such as Nick's receiving banana cream pie instead of cheesecake).

In Stage Twelve, we *commune:* we commune with ourselves, with the Source, with the Earth, and with one another. The result is unity; not necessarily unity of opinion, but unity in our intent to commune. Unity without communion, unity without divergence of opinion, unity without our shadows and without our gifts may involve the phenomenon of a physical community, but not the consciousness of the twelfth stage of healing.

Divergent energies are necessary for successful community because it is only through challenging our patterns and perspectives that we can learn to live more deeply within ourselves, move past our wounds, and relinquish old, less functional ways. Through diversity we can establish a community that involves merging with divergent energies. Like the process of healing the bodymind by accepting the reality of dissonant regions within us, a community is able to achieve a higher level of evolution and order.

Ritual and Community

The term *spiritual* comprises two words we are familiar with: "spiral" and "ritual." Both are aspects of community. The healing journey may be compared to a spiral staircase, and ritual is often a function of Community.

Many ancient and traditional societies have established rituals to honor the cyclic and periodic chaos of the natural world, such as volcanic eruptions, storms, tornados, and earthquakes. Participation in these ceremonies acts as a focal point for the community. In these rituals, individuals bring their uniqueness and their gifts; they share both their shadows and their light. Ritual violence, name-calling, and expressions of fear, rage, respect, generosity, and longing are often integral aspects of such ceremonies, which acknowledge the shadow in order to move beyond it.

As we have said, few rituals remain in Western industrialized society. It is difficult to accept our shadow and our light without support from social models. As a result, our energy becomes repressed and seeks to be discharged. With a loss of individual power and no known vehicles to learn the rhythms of the twelve stages, violent and criminal behavior are often the consequence. Oddly enough, the treatment of criminals and others with "antisocial" behavior is indeed ritualistic.

Expressing The Energy of Community

In the stage of Community, we are aware that everything is interconnected and interpenetrating. We cannot escape our connection with Universal Law. The Buddhists call this the Law of Karma; in physics it is the law of cause and effect. Oren Lyons, a Native American chief, said, "There is a universal law. As we obey the law, we prosper; as we ignore the law, we suffer. But there is no discussion with universal law."

In Stage Eleven, we realized that a major task of humanity is to channel energy constructively. We also understood that the life force is a precious gift and we want to use it wisely. The desire to express this force springs from a cellular understanding of the true nature of existence. This understanding is the natural result of moving through the previous healing stages.

In the Twelfth Stage, Community, we strive to find ways for how we may best focus and express this energy to further unity, respect, and planetary healing. As a result, alignment with this energy produces profound shifts in consciousness as we move through Stage Twelve. For example, in Stage Four, we may have chosen not to eat meat because we felt it might make us sick. In Stage Six, we may have decided not to eat it because of its high animal fat content; in stages Ten or Eleven, we may have experienced the pain and suffering of the billions of animals that are factory-farmed and slaughtered for food. By the time we enter Stage Twelve, we have expanded our perspective of community to include the animals that are killed for food.

We may feel that killing animals for food violates the spiritual energy that expresses itself through them. We may realize that our choice of eating meat perpetuates suffering and cruelty. We may also take into account the tremendous amount of energy required to enjoy an animal-based diet and realize that eating so high on the food chain is an inefficient use of spiritual energy. As our circle or perspective of life becomes larger and larger, we realize that all animals share a common force of life and that maintaining captive animals and killing them for food becomes almost as offensive as killing our pet dogs or cats for food.

I choose to mention animal consumption because it is an excellent example of the way in which our choices impact the larger world community. We are not accustomed to seeing the interconnection and interdependence of our animal consumption on the global picture. Our society's consciousness is one that protects us from involvement in the world. It is not one that encourages us to make choices. It does not support the question, "Do we really need this?"

But by the time we reach Stage Twelve, we have no difficulty questioning our choices. Nothing is excluded. Because we participate in this world, in the middle of our usual activities, our customary meals, or our ordinary purchases, we experience a deep voice within that asks, "What the heck are you doing?" We know that no matter how annoying the voice is, we cannot hide from it.

In Stage Twelve, a simple choice such as what we will have for dinner becomes important. All our choices affect community. Therefore, even making a small change, at any point it feels appropriate, can have a significant affect. This does not mean that if we are in Stage Twelve, we must become a vegetarian. But we might ask, "Am I using vital energy wisely?" We may also become more aware of how we use our money (green energy) and explore how it can be used to promote wholeness and healing by the goods and services we purchase and the contributions we make.

We may become more aware of how we waste our personal energy through arguments,worrying, indulging in distractions, or living on the periphery. We may realize how we tend to withhold our energy by not helping others who are in need. We may want to conserve Earth energy through eating a plant-based diet, recycling, and avoiding products that use high amounts of energy in their manufacture. No matter what aspects of life we consider, we recognize that the choices we make either support healing or don't.

We Are Each Other's Medicine

Community can also be good for our health. Studies have shown that the interpersonal support found in community helps keep people healthier and can even prolong one's life. The book *Creating Community Anywhere* spoke of the findings of Dr. Dean Ornish, the noted cardiologist. In his work with heart patients, he found that support groups — which promoted intimacy and the sharing of feelings — were as important as the dietary, exercise, and stress reduction techniques he recommended for his patients.

The Sunrise Ranch, one of a dozen Emissary communities, is an example of an intentional community. Members believe that diversity is an essential aspect of community and they consistently attune with one another, which involves connecting themselves to the energy or source. Nick Gordon said, "In community, I feel we are each other's medicine." He refers to our gifts of individuality that we share both with ourselves and with others in the larger community.

Recognizing that in community we are "each other's medicine" is fundamental in both our inner community and in the world community. In our inner community, our body produces antibiotics, insulin, pain medication, chemicals to achieve altered states of consciousness, and other elements we need to grow, heal, and function. The bodymind produces everything we need in exact amounts, provided that its internal communication lines are free from interference. As a result, our body can express the perfection of the indwelling spirit that forms the core of our existence. We are our own medicine.

The same process takes place in marriage, with our children, in the workplace, and in our neighborhood, city, national, and international communities when we have this realization. We are each other's medicine. We bring our gifts to each other. But first we must be available to ourselves. When we have moved through the later stages of healing, we realize that everyone in our sphere of consciousness is there to provide us with the gift of light or shadow to empower us to further activate our own healing process.

Moving Through the Stages

Most people live the majority of their lives in the early stages of healing. In fact, some people may spend their entire lives shuttling between stages One and Two, with occasional short visits to stages Three and Four. Stages One and Two become their baseline of reality.

Although initially we may spend the majority of our time in stages Two and Three and less in the later stages, as we move into stages Eight through Twelve, the equation changes. We begin to spend very little of our time in the early stages and the majority of our time in the later stages.

In our healing journey, we must move through all the different stages. Once we have journeyed through all of the stages in order, we may revisit any stage out of sequence. With the Twelve Stage model presented in this book (and provided that we can ascertain which stage we are in), we now have the tools to utilize the movements, breathing exercises, and declarations of any stage. As a result, these tools help us to unify with that stage, learn the lessons it has to offer, and move to our new baseline stage of healing.

Commitment to Community

In Stage Twelve, we naturally and joyously commit to the spirit of community, whether it is the community of the bodymind, a primary relationship, the neighborhood, or the world. Unlike Stage Ten, we realize we do not come to the stage of Community just to visit. We arrive at this stage from the commitment we made in Stage Eleven, as the result of recognizing our connection with the world and acknowledging our responsibility to participate in the world community or the community we include in our circle.

Committing to actions that resonate with the later stages of healing is what community is about. The consciousness of community has an energy and rhythm of its own, and it fills us and guides us further on our journey of healing, wholeness, and discovery.

The image of an oak tree offers a perfect example of an individual in community. Like the oak, our healing process empowers us to be strong and grounded, with our roots growing deeper into the earth while our perspectives expand and reach toward the heavens. By being grounded in Mother Earth, which includes connecting with her life force, chaos, nourishment, and wisdom, we receive the gifts the world has to offer. And like the tree, which offers its gifts of oxygen, shelter, strength, grace, beauty, and abundance, we offer our gifts to others.

The more we heal the more we grow. We become stronger, wiser, more loving, and more forgiving. Like the large, majestic oak, we become a "pillar of the community" in which we live. In Stage Twelve, we commit ourselves to community, yet we do so with humility, grace, openness, and dedication. There can be no greater commitment and no greater gift: to serve as a channel to assist in personal and planetary healing.

Hearing Yourself Ask for Help

"Please help me find within myself the gifts I have not given to myself." "Please make suffering easier for me this time." "Please help me bring my gifts to others and allow others to bring their gifts to me." "Please let me experience others as they truly are." These are some of the requests we may make when we experience ourselves in Stage Twelve.

Stage Twelve Exercise

Stand with your feet a comfortable distance apart with your arms at your sides. Bend forward, hands between your legs with palms toward the ground and fingertips barely touching the ground. Breathe in through your nose. Bring your arms to your upper thighs as you straighten up. Raise your arms toward your head and begin to exhale as you reach your heart center. As you move your hands up with palms toward the ceiling, arch your back, move your head back slightly and look up. Now exhale slowly through your mouth with a vowel sound, like "Ahhh" or "Ohhh." As your hands reach upwards, connect to the energy of the "stars."

Bring your hands from the top of your head down over your face washing your face in the "star" energy. Bring your hands down your body toward your heart. When you reach the heart center, inhale again. As you inhale, continue moving your hands down to your feet so that you are again in a position to take a breath in. It is like letting water fall over your body; you are cleansing yourself in the waterfall of light and spirit. Exhale and repeat the exercise.

As you bring your hands toward the ground, you are honoring the Earth energy and breathing in the substance of the Earth. As you raise your body, you are moving up and breathing out to the heavens. You then wash yourself with the perfection of your love and spirit and bring it back to the Earth again.

Visualize where you draw your circle of interconnectedness, responsibility, and experience. Bless your circle and all who are within it.

Stage Twelve Declarations

"I give my gifts and I receive other's gifts."

"I find the gifts I have denied myself and I give my gifts to others."

"I am one with the web of life."

"My circle of love and learning expands just perfectly."

Stage Twelve Exercise

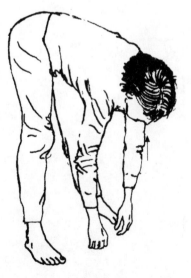
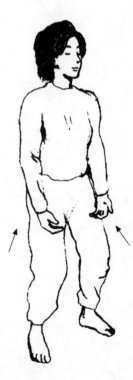

Afterword

Your rhythm is your truth and it shall set you free.

Aesop told the story of an old farmer who realized that he was about to die. He wanted to share the secrets that are naturally passed from an elder to his children. He called them over and said, "My sons, I am shortly about to die. I would have you know, therefore, that in my vineyard lies hidden treasure. Dig and you will find it."

As soon as the father died, the sons took their shovels, spades, and pitchforks and dug throughout the vineyard searching for the hidden treasure. They turned and churned every inch of soil for many days, but no buried treasure could be found. However, by the time of harvest a plentiful and magnificent crop of succulent grapes filled the vineyard, the likes of which had never been seen before. Aesop's moral to the fable? "There is no treasure without toil."

In this story, the riches that the sons received were both different from, and more plentiful than, they expected. When we commit ourselves to serving the process of life, knowing that a treasure lies — however elusive — in every circumstance, then life will mysteriously, miraculously (and often chaotically) bring us gifts. These gifts are invariably more plentiful and varied than we have asked for, and are more likely to be bestowed upon us when we live our lives spontaneously, without attempting to understand the meaning of everything or seeking to control what we do not like or do not yet comprehend.

By moving through The Twelve Stages of Healing, we gradually learn that we no longer take life, events, situations, and other people so personally. Life provides us with lessons which can be difficult until we no longer resist them, but instead, resonate with them. This means resonating with the consciousness of the inner rhythms of life, rather than identifying with their outer form or manifestation.

The toil that we perform in life does not always need to be unpleasant. When we are in harmony with our rhythms, the work or toil we perform becomes natural to us. This is just as natural as a sneeze, taking a shower, or riding a bicycle. Most likely, it will be others observing our toil (and who are in a different rhythm than we are) who will perceive it as being difficult or unpleasant. Life gives us whatever we require when the rhythm of the consciousness we need to express takes over our physiology and our psyche.

Over the years, I have watched thousands of individuals moving along their healing process and move through all Twelve Stages of Healing. I have been through these stages myself many times, and continue to experience them in my own daily life. I also know that healing does not belong to any one approach, be it chiropractic, acupuncture, traditional medicine, Somato-Respiratory Integration, bioenergetics, or any other modality. Healing is simply an expression of life unfolding toward a higher order of complexity and consciousness.

As you journey through The Twelve Stages of Healing, know that your experiences — whatever they may be — are valid. You no longer need to figure your way out of the stage you have been in, or think your way into the next healing stage. As you connect with yourself in the ways described in each chapter, you naturally become more aware, more alive, more whole, and more *you!*

The consciousness that gives your brain, heart, lungs, stomach, gall bladder, and all the rest of you its rhythms is the same "stuff" that stands behind the universal processes of creation, growth, and healing. Strive to synchronize yourself with these natural rhythms and let them dance with you. Embrace your rhythms and let them embrace you. Your rhythm is your truth, and your truth will set you free.

When it becomes natural and effortless for you to be at any stage of consciousness, to be one with its rhythm, you've gotten it. Life then moves you on into another stage for you to learn more, somewhat like a dancer rehearsing and rehearsing until the dancer and the dance become one. Your organic rhythms are one with your rhythms of consciousness. You know when you are there. It doesn't last long, but neither does going through any door or gateway. This is where the treasure lies — beyond your present state of awareness.

In the Introduction, I mentioned that *The Twelve Stages of Healing* will guide you through your healing journey. New information and ideas that parallel your newly achieved levels of awareness will suddenly jump out as you read (and re-read) this book. By studying and working with this book, I hope that you now have a clearer picture of where you are now, where you have been, and where you are going on this magical journey of transformation. With the knowledge you have gained, you can now distinguish your suffering from your pain, your ascent from your light behind the form, your emptiness from your preparation for resolution. You may be aware of when you are stuck in a perspective, and be OK about it, without feeling you must do something about it. You now know that it is not necessary to identify with the phenomenon, but instead appreciate the consciousness that the phenomenon may help produce.

Once you have passed through all Twelve Stages of Healing, you may no longer need the acute physical or emotional symptoms you may have experienced before to advise you of the need to change. For example, you may be in Stage One (Suffering), and have an awareness that "I am helpless now, nothing works for me" without experiencing any physical pain. This is not to say that you will always be comfortable as you move again and again through The Twelve Stages of Healing —far from it! Yet, as the rhythms and messages found in each stage become more clear to you, you will continually enjoy new insights and levels of wholeness you never experienced before.

I encourage everyone reading these pages to consider healing as a responsibility, a gift, and a birthright. If you need to step off the healing path from time to time to gain more comfort, relief, or necessary treatment, do it proudly. Ask for help from within yourself, from others, and from your spiritual source, in whatever form or model works for you at the time. Strive to devote at least as much attention to removing interference to the expression of your innate rhythms and intelligence as you have to the effects that these blockages have had on your life and its movement.

Finally, I encourage you to read fairy tales, biblical stories, and myths and legends from all traditions of the human community. Investigate the ancient and the indigenous expressions of life from around the world. Embrace the journey, and you may live happily ever after. . .

Bibliographic Index

Preface

Bettleheim, Bruno. *The Uses of Enchantment.* New York: Vintage Books, 1977, p. 25.

Introduction

Bendit, Laurence J. *The Mysteries Today.* London: The Theosophical Publishing House, 1973, p. 71.

Kunz, Dora, ed. *Spiritual Aspects of the Healing Arts.* Wheaton, IL: Quest Books, 1989, p. 87, 117.

Kurtz, Ernest, and Katherine Ketcham. *The Spirituality of Imperfection.* New York: Bantam Books, 1992, p. 31.

Chapter One

Assagioli, Roberto. *Psychosynthesis.* New York: Penguin Books, 1976, p. 87.

Bettleheim, Bruno. *Uses of Enchantment.* p. 183–93.

Collins Cobuild English Language Dictionary. London: William Collins Sons, 1987, p. 1034.

Grimm's Complete Fairy Tales. Garden City, NY: International Collectors Library, 1983, p. 95–6.

Jerry Howard and Jeff Wagenheim, editors, "Men on Midlife." *New Age Journal.* (July/August 1993).

Raheem, Aminah. *Soul Return.* Aptos, CA: Aminah Raheem, 1987, p. 172.

Roberts, Bernadette. *The Path to No-Self.* Boston: Shambhala Publications, 1985, p. 9.

Schimmel, Annemarie. *Mystical Dimensions of Islam.* University of North Carolina Press, 1975, p. 137.

Walker, Benjamin. *The Hindu World. Vol. 2.* New York: Frederick A. Praeger, 1968, p. 446.

Webster's Ninth New Collegiate Dictionary. Springfield, MA: Merriam-Webster, 1983, p. 1179.

Chapter Two

Capra, Fritjof. *The Turning Point*. New York: Simon and Schuster, 1982, p. 28.

Cole, Joanna. *Best Loved Folktales of the World*. New York: Anchor Books, 1983, p. 468–9.

Donden, Yeshi. *Health Through Balance*. Ithaca, NY: Snow Lion Publications, 1986, p. 37.

Eliade, Mircea, ed., *The Encyclopedia of Religion*, Vol. 14, New York: Macmillan, 1987, p. 100.

Kunz, Dora, ed. *Spiritual Aspects of the Healing Arts*, p. 59.

Nicholson, Shirley. *Ancient Wisdom, Modern Insight*. Wheaton, IL: Quest Books, 1985, p. 100.

Chapter Three

Altman, Nathaniel. *Everybody's Guide to Chiropractic Health Care*. Los Angeles: Jeremy P. Tarcher, 1990, p. 79–82.

Bradshaw, John. *Bradshaw On: The Family*. Deerfield Beach, FL: Health Communications, 1988, p. 74–5.

Chopra, Deepak. *Quantum Healing*. New York: Bantam Books, 1989, p. 48–9.

Lowen, Alexander. *Depression and the Body*. New York: Pelican Books, 1980, p. 260–1, 267.

Pierrakos, John. *Core Energetics*. Mendocino, CA: LifeRhythm Publications, 1987, p. 88.

Chapter Four

Assagioli, Roberto. *Psychosynthesis*. p. 39.

Pierrakos, John C. *Bulletin & Pathwords*. May 1979, p. 52.

Cole, Joanna. *Best Loved Folktales*. p. 97.

Lemkov, Anna. *The Wholeness Principle*. Wheaton, IL: Quest Books, 1990, p. 116.

Taber's Cyclopedic Medical Dictionary. Philadelphia: F.A. Davis, 1977, p. 34.

Chapter Five

Alexander, Hartley Burr. *The World's Rim*. University of Nebraska Press, 1967, p. 136–69.

Bailey, Alice A. *Esoteric Psychology*. Vol. 2. New York: Lucis Publishing, 1970, p. 312.

Campbell, Don, ed. *Music and Miracles*. Wheaton, IL: Quest Books, 1992, p. 65–6.

Cole, Joanna. *Best Loved Folktales*. p. 8–23.

Kurtz, Ernest, and Katherine Ketcham. *Spirituality of Imperfection*. p. 38–9, 40.

Roberts, Bernadette. *The Path to No-Self*. p. 9–10.

Chapter Six

Dossey, Larry. *Space, Time and Medicine*. Boulder: Shambhala Publications, 1982, p. 183.

Chapter Seven

Grimm's Complete Fairy Tales. p. 4.

Dethlefsen, Thorwald, and Rudiger Dahlke, M.D. *The Healing Power of Illness*. Rockport, MA: Element Books, 1991, p. 9.

Krishnamurti, J. *The First and Last Freedom*. Wheaton, IL: Quest Books, 1968, p. 111–14.

Smith, Fritz Frederick. *Inner Bridges*. Atlanta: Humanics New Age, 1987, p. 175.

Chapter Eight

Allen, Marc. *Tantra for the West*. San Rafael, CA: New World Library, 1992, p. 86.

Best Loved Bible Stories. Chicago: World Book-Childcraft International, 1980, p. 100–04.

Brown, Patricia Leigh. "Time to Go." *The New York Times*. Sec. 9, p. 1. 26 September 1993.

Campbell, Don G. *The Roar of Silence*. Wheaton, IL: Quest Books, 1989.

Perry, Danaan, *The Essence Book of Days*.

Roth, David. *May the Light of Love*. New York: MaytheLight Music, 1988.

Schimmel, Annemarie. *Mystical Dimensions Islam*. p. 162.

Talbot, Michael. *Beyond the Quantum*. New York, Macmillan, 1986, p. 156.

Trepp, Leo. *Eternal Faith Eternal People*, Englewood Cliffs, NJ: Prentice-Hall, 1962, p. 187–95.

Zambucka, Kristin. *The Keepers of the Earth*. Honolulu: Harrame Publishing, 1984, p. 58.

Chapter Nine

Bondi, Julia, and Nathaniel Altman. *Lovelight*. New York: Pocket Books, 1989, p. 71–2.

Brennan, Barbara Ann. *Hands of Light*. New York: Bantam Books, 1987.

Leadbeater, C.W. *The Chakras*. Wheaton, IL: Quest Books, 1987.

Redfield, James. *The Celestine Prophecy*. Hoover, AL: Satori Publishing, 1993, p. 51–3.

Sheldrake, Rupert. *The Rebirth of Nature*. New York: Bantam Books, 1991, p. 98.

Yogananda, Paramahansa. *Whispers for Eternity*. Los Angeles: Self-Realization Fellowship, 1959.

Chapter Ten

Castaneda, Carlos. *Tales of Power*. New York, Simon and Schuster, 1974, p. 283–4.

Eccles, Sir John et al. *The Reach of the Mind*. Dallas: Saybrook Publishing, 1985, p. 56–7.

Hastings, Arthur. *With the Tongues of Men and Angels*. Ft. Worth: Holt, Rhinehart and Winston, 1991, p. 186–7, 189.

The Holy Bible. New York: The New York Bible Society.

Kriyananda [J. Donald Walters]. *The Essence of Self-Realization*. Nevada City, CA: Crystal Clarity Publishers, 1990, p. 153.

Raheem, Aminah. *Soul Return*. p. 172.

Roberts, Bernadette. *The Path to No-Self*. p. 43.

Thweatt, Charley. Santa Cruz, CA: Angellight Music.

Chapter Eleven

Bodian, Stephan. "A Path With a Heart." *Yoga Journal*. (November/December 1993): p. 59.

Bailey, Alice A. *A Treatise on White Magic*. New York: Lucis Publishing, 1970, p. 99.

Campbell, Joseph. *Myths to Live By*. New York: Bantam Books, 1972, p. 266–7.

Complete Works of Pir-o-Murshid Hazrat Inayat Khan, 1923 I:

January–June. London: East-West Publications, 1989.

Cohen, Alan. *Going Bonkers.* December 1993, p. 7.

Gordon, Nick. Interview with author. 16 October 1993.

H.H. The Dalai Lama [Gyatso, Tenzin]. *Ocean of Wisdom.* Santa Fe: Clear Light Publishers, 1989, p. 59.

Justice, Blair. *Who Gets Sick?* Los Angeles: Jeremy P. Tarcher, 1988, p. 266–7.

Shah, Idries. *The Way of the Sufi.* New York: E.P. Dutton, 1970, p. 186.

Toms, Michael. "Magical Thinking: An Interview with Deepak Chopra, M.D." *New Dimensions* (January–February, 1992): 6–7.

Trungpa, Chogyam. Shambhala: *The Sacred Path of the Warrior.* Boulder: Shambhala Publications, 1984, p. 85.

Chapter Twelve

Cole, Joanna. *Best Loved Folktales.* p. 8, 23, 78, 485.

Earthsave Foundation. *Our Food, Our World.* Santa Cruz: Earthsave Foundation, 1992.

Gordon, Nick. Interview with author. 15 October 1993.

Harman, Willis W. "The Transpersonal Challenge to the Scientific Paradigm: The Need for a Restructuring of Science." *ReVISION*, 11, no. 2 (Fall 1988): 13–21.

Houston, Jean. "The Sacred Wound." *TANTRA: The Magazine.* Green Tara. (1993): 46.

Grimm's Complete Fairy Tales. p. 96.

Kurtz, Ernest, and Katherine Ketcham. *Spirituality of Imperfection.* p. 47.

McLaughlin, Corrine, and Gordon Davidson. *Builders of the Dawn.* Summertown, TN: The Book Publishing, 1989, p. 9.

Shaffer, Carolyn R. and Kristin Anundsen. *Creating Community Anywhere.* New York: J. P. Tarcher/Perigee, 1993, p. 321–322.

About the Authors

Donny Epstein is the founder and developer of Somato Respiratory Integration and Network Spinal Analysis, both revolutionary modalities promoting enhanced well-being.

A 1977 graduate of New York Chiropractic College, Dr. Epstein created two successful practices in New York, where he first began developing his models of health, healing and wellness. In the early 1980s he began teaching wellness, developmental and transformational programs, which he now teaches internationally to thousands of practitioners.

Dr. Epstein's methodologies are researched at universities, have been published extensively in professional journals, incorporated into post graduate programs in several disciplines and have been featured on television, magazines and newspapers around the world. Dr. Epstein serves on several boards, and has also presented testimony to the White House Commission of Complimentary and Alternative Medicine.

For those seeking revolutionary and practical means of advancing their human condition, Dr. Donald Epstein has been considered for over 25 years to be one of the true visionaries of growth and human potential.

Dr. Epstein lives in Boulder, Colorado with his wife Jackie. They together are committed to creating a global change through the transformation of individuals, families, communities and nations. They have four children Daniel, David, Debra and Louise, as well as 5 delightful grandchildren Daniel, Donovan, Anika, Savannah and Ryan.

Nathaniel Altman has written over fifteen books on diet, philosophy, and holistic health. His titles include *Everybody's Guide to Chiropractic Health Care* (Tarcher, 1990), *What You Can Do About Asthma* (Dell, 1991), and *Sacred Trees* (Sierra Club Books, 1994). He lives in Brooklyn, New York.

For information about The Twelve Stages of Healing workshops,
video and DVDs of the Somato-Respiratory Integration exercises,
and other support materials, contact:

Wise World Seminars
444 North Main Street
Longmont, CO 80501
(303) 678-8086
http://www.wiseworldseminars.com

Also from Amber-Allen Publishing

Healing Myths, Healing Magic by Donald M. Epstein. Dr. Epstein examines the deeply ingrained stories, or "myths," we commonly hold about how our bodies heal — myths that can actually inhibit healing. He then suggests an alternative statement, or *Healing Magic,* to help us reclaim our body's natural ability to heal.

Creating Affluence by Deepak Chopra. With clear and simple wisdom, Deepak Chopra explores the full meaning of wealth consciousness and presents simple A-to-Z steps that spontaneously generate wealth in all its forms.*

Dreams, "Evolution," and Value Fulfillment, Volumes One and Two by Jane Roberts. These two volumes answer crucial questions about the entire significance of Seth's system of thought and take us on a journey to identify the origins of our universe and our species.

The Four Agreements by don Miguel Ruiz. Based on ancient Toltec wisdom, the Four Agreements offer a powerful code of conduct that can rapidly transform our lives to a new experience of freedom, true happiness, and love.

The Four Agreements Companion Book by don Miguel Ruiz with Janet Mills. This book offers additional insights, practice ideas, a dialogue with don Miguel about applying the Four Agreements, and true stories from people who have transformed their lives.

The Individual and the Nature of Mass Events by Jane Roberts. Extending the idea that we create our own reality, Seth explores the connection between personal beliefs and world events.

The Magical Approach by Jane Roberts. Seth discusses how we can live our lives spontaneously, creatively, and according to our own natural rhythms.*

The Mastery of Love by don Miguel Ruiz. This book illuminates the fear-based beliefs and assumptions that undermine love and lead to suffering and drama in our relationships. Using insightful stories, Ruiz shows us how to heal our emotional wounds, recover the freedom and joy that are our birthright, and restore the spirit of playfulness that is vital to loving relationships.

The Nature of Personal Reality by Jane Roberts. Seth explains how the conscious mind directs unconscious activity, and has at its command all the powers of the inner self.*

The Nature of the Psyche by Jane Roberts. Seth reveals a startling new concept of self, answering questions about many aspects of the psyche, including love, dreams, sexuality, and death.

The Oversoul Seven Trilogy by Jane Roberts. The adventures of Oversoul Seven are an intriguing fantasy, a mind-altering exploration of our being, and a vibrant celebration of life.

Seth Speaks by Jane Roberts. In this essential guide to conscious living, Seth clearly and powerfully articulates the concept that we create our own reality according to our beliefs.*

The Seven Spiritual Laws of Success by Deepak Chopra. In this classic international bestseller, Deepak Chopra distills the essence of his teachings into seven simple, yet powerful principles that can easily be applied to create success in all areas of our lives.*

The "Unknown" Reality, Volumes One and Two by Jane Roberts. Exploring the interdependence of multiple selves, Seth explains how understanding unknown dimensions can change the world as we know it.

The Voice of Knowledge by don Miguel Ruiz with Janet Mills. In this breakthrough book, don Miguel Ruiz shows us how to recover our faith in the truth and return to our own common sense. He changes the way we perceive ourselves and the way we perceive other people. Then he opens the door to a reality that we once perceived when we were one or two years old — a reality of truth, love, and joy.

The Way Toward Health by Jane Roberts. Woven through the poignant story of Jane Roberts' final days are Seth's teachings about self-healing and the mind's effect upon physical health.

Living Beyond Miracles by Deepak Chopra and Wayne Dyer (Audio CD). Deepak Chopra and Wayne Dyer collaborate for the first time on this remarkable audio. Recorded before a live audience, this dynamic presentation features individual talks by the two men, followed by their fascinating and inspiring conversation about the search for self-discovery.*

Living Without Limits by Deepak Chopra and Wayne Dyer (Audio CD). Two leaders in the field of human potential share their wisdom before a live audience as they question and challenge one another on the importance of quieting the inner dialogue, the power we have to heal ourselves of fatal diseases, the negative impact of the media on our health, and more.

*Co-published by Amber-Allen Publishing and New World Library.

This book is co-published by Amber-Allen Publishing
and New World Library.

For a catalog of New World Library titles, contact:

NEW WORLD LIBRARY
14 Pamaron Way
Novato, CA 94949

Phone: (415) 884-2100 ext. 50
Fax: (415) 884-2199

To purchase additional copies of this book,
call toll free: (800) 972-6657

Visit our website at www.nwlib.com

For a catalog of Amber-Allen titles, contact:

AMBER-ALLEN PUBLISHING
Post Office Box 6657
San Rafael, CA 94903

Fax: (415) 499-3174

To place an order, call toll-free:
(800) 624-8855

Visit our website at www.amberallen.com